Richard church.

FOR POTTERY & PEACE

FOR POTTERY & PEACE

A Northampton Family Story

~

Richard Church

Matador
9 Priory Business Park,
Wistow Road, Kibworth Beauchamp,
Leicestershire LE8 0RX
Tel: 0116 279 2299
Email: books@troubador.co.uk
Web: www.troubador.co.uk/matador
Twitter: @matadorbooks

ISBN 978 1838591 717

British Library Cataloguing in Publication Data.
A catalogue record for this book is available from the British Library.

Printed and bound by CPI Group (UK) Ltd, Croydon, CR0 4YY
Typeset in 11pt Adobe Garamond Pro by Troubador Publishing Ltd, Leicester, UK

Matador is an imprint of Troubador Publishing Ltd

CONTENTS

ACKNOWLEDGEMENTS

This book is rather unexpected. For several years I had been researching my family's history. Like thousands of others, I had used online genealogy resources to confirm the bare bones of what I knew about my family and had added to that knowledge by going further back and wider. Later I was able to add to my knowledge with the digitisation of old newspapers online through the British Library's online British Newspapers Archive.

A few years ago, packing boxes of supposed rubbish to be taken to the recycling centre, a bundle of faded papers caught my eye. They were my grandfather's typed transcription of my great uncle's diaries of First World War experiences as a conscientious objector. I knew they existed, and I knew they were important, and they were saved just in time. Our history often hangs on such fragile threads.

A very belated thank you is due both to my grandfather Wilfrid and my great uncle William, without whom this book would have been much shorter. I think William and Wilfrid Church both expected their diaries to be read and used after they died. We have left it a while, but I hope this book would meet their expectations.

Wilfrid's diaries are not all that he left behind. In 1967 he wrote a little booklet 'A Record of an old-established Retail China & Glass

Business' and shared it with family, friends and people in the china and glass industry. Most of that booklet is reproduced throughout this book.

Other resources have helped with the story of the family during the First World War, including the Peace Pledge Union's online project www.menwhosaidno.org, the Imperial War Museum website and the Dartmoor Trust website. John Buckell used William's diaries in writing 'Sacrifice, Service & Survival- Weston Favell in the First World War', and in so doing uncovered additional information that contributed to the chapter on the First World War.

I was fortunate that the village of East Ilsley, where this book opens, has an excellent local history group that has published some fascinating material. The booklet 'A drunken worthless creature', by Kay Sanderson supplied the comments of the local vicar with which this book begins.

Northampton Chess club have provided material on Wesley and William's involvement in their Club and let me take a photograph of their Church Cup.

The memories of my parents and my siblings have all helped with the book. Wherever possible I have always tried to verify personal memories with other evidence, and in most cases I have been able to. My father Vivian Church's memories have turned out to be remarkably accurate.

I am grateful to all the members of my family for their support and encouragement in writing this book. To my Mother, my sister Katie and my brother Stephen for their comments and suggestions on the first draft, and for their help with editing the later draft.

Church Family Tree

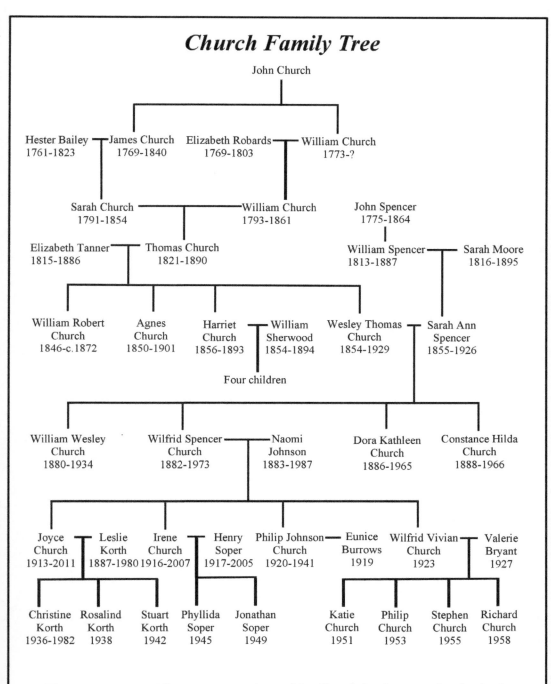

John Church

Hester Bailey 1761-1823 — James Church 1769-1840   Elizabeth Robards 1769-1803 — William Church 1773-?

Sarah Church 1791-1854   William Church 1793-1861   John Spencer 1775-1864

Elizabeth Tanner 1815-1886 — Thomas Church 1821-1890   William Spencer 1813-1887 — Sarah Moore 1816-1895

William Robert Church 1846-c.1872   Agnes Church 1850-1901   Harriet Church 1856-1893 — William Sherwood 1854-1894   Wesley Thomas Church 1854-1929 — Sarah Ann Spencer 1855-1926

Four children

William Wesley Church 1880-1934   Wilfrid Spencer Church 1882-1973 — Naomi Johnson 1883-1987   Dora Kathleen Church 1886-1965   Constance Hilda Church 1888-1966

Joyce Church 1913-2011 — Leslie Korth 1887-1980   Irene Church 1916-2007 — Henry Soper 1917-2005   Philip Johnson Church 1920-1941 — Eunice Burrows 1919   Wilfrid Vivian Church 1923 — Valerie Bryant 1927

Christine Korth 1936-1982   Rosalind Korth 1938   Stuart Korth 1942   Phyllida Soper 1945   Jonathan Soper 1949   Katie Church 1951   Philip Church 1953   Stephen Church 1955   Richard Church 1958

This is a summary of the seven generations of the Church family covered in this book.

It does not include all of the offspring from every generation.

CHAPTER ONE

THE RANTERS

THE YEAR WAS 1831. THE REV. THOMAS LOVEDAY HAS BEEN appointed as the new rector of the village of East Ilsley, a large rural parish on the Berkshire Downs. Settling into his new home, he opened the drawer on his desk to find a little notebook with some kind words left by his predecessor the Rev. George Thomas.

Mr Thomas had been the vicar for 22 years and he knew everyone in the village well. He knew about their work, their homes and their families. Most of all he knew whether they came to his church or went elsewhere for Sunday worship. His notes gave his successor a helpful pen picture of each parishioner, coupled with a map to show where they all lived. He was blunt in his opinions. One parishioner being described as a 'drunken worthless creature', another 'wife slovenly, seldom at church'.

Many of the villagers attended non-conformist meetings, and some attended both church and chapel. Mr Thomas reported that some people were rarely or never seen at church, several of these he described as 'Ranters', a nickname for followers of Primitive Methodism.

The vicar had a problem with Methodists. An itinerant Primitive Methodist preacher by the name of Elizabeth Smith had preached on

Ilsley Downs the previous year. Her success had caught the attention of another Methodist preacher, Thomas Russell, whom she later married. Thomas wrote in his diary on 29th January 1831:

> *'Visited and preached at East Ilsley. Miss Smith first came here; but a vile man came up, and swore that none of us should preach here; but she believed the Lord could turn the lion into a lamb; and it was so, for conviction seized his conscience, and he turned to the Lord.'*

James Church was probably not this vile man, but It is likely that he was known to Elizabeth Smith and Thomas Russell. James was someone the Rev. Thomas kept an eye on, describing him in his notes: *'Tailor. The head of the Methodists, large family. Ranter'*. He was born in East Ilsley in 1771. At the age of 15 he was apprenticed to a tailor, Thomas Bailey. It seems that the apprenticeship was successful, for in 1790 he married Thomas's younger sister Hester, and set up his own tailoring business.

James's younger brother William had left East Ilsley to live in Cholsey, a small village just ten miles away on the Thames. The Reading Mercury and Oxford Gazette of Monday 9th April 1798 reported that fundraising was under way throughout the land for the defence of the nation against France. In the village of Cholsey *'Free gifts'* are listed *'In Aid of the subscription of the Bank of England, for the Defence of this Country against an inveterate and implacable foe'*. The 35 donations are ordered by size, the largest was £30. Three up from the bottom, there was the sum of 1s 6d donated by Mr Church. This is the first known newspaper record of the family.

On 29th March 1817 brothers James and William came together for a wedding in East Ilsley. William's son, also called William, married Sarah, James's eldest daughter. It was not uncommon in those times for cousins to marry. William and Sarah Church settled in East Ilsley, not far from Sarah's father. The young couple had also caught the attention of Reverend Thomas, who had this advice for his successor in the rectory.

'Journeyman carpenter to Pointer. Lives with T. Finch. Preacher of Methodists but very steady. 4 in family *footnote: William Church every Sunday distributes pamphlets which should be checked by better ones of yours.'

Maybe the advice was to produce better pamphlets to check the influence of William Church, or alternatively to check the contents of William's pamphlets. As a journeyman William had completed his carpentry apprenticeship and was qualified to work for Henry Poynter on a daily wage.

East Ilsley was a large village. The 1848 Kelly's directory of Berkshire refers to the huge sheep fairs held throughout the year, the largest being in August, when it is said that 50,000 sheep were sold. In October there was a fair unfortunately described as 'for the hiring of servants and pleasure'. What is now a quiet village must then have been a bustling community.

The Kelly's directory lists 51 traders in the village, including William Church, wheelwright, living 'near the pond'. The pond is still there today. In the 1851 census he was living in Abingdon Rd, described as a wheelwright, carpenter and smith employing three men. He had become a successful local tradesman, to have an entry in a countywide directory required some local status.

William died in 1861, leaving a will which is recorded in the national probate calendar as being 'under £600', but that is a sizeable sum for a rural craftsman in the mid-19th century. William and Sarah are both buried in East Ilsley churchyard, their methodism did not prevent their burial on ground consecrated by the Church of England.

Thomas Church

The third and only surviving son of William and Sarah had the most to gain from inheritance. In 1844 Thomas married Elizabeth Tanner, the daughter of a shoemaker from Ecchinswell in Hampshire. In 1847 he is listed in the Post Office directory as a grocer in East Ilsley and his wife as a straw bonnet maker. He moved on from grocery. In the 1851 census he is listed as a draper and carpenter, living in Abingdon Rd, East Ilsley with his wife, still a straw bonnet maker.

Generations of Churches had lived in East Ilsley, but by the middle of the nineteenth century the arrival of the railways saw many families drawn away from their rural homes and move to towns in search of a better life. On November 6th, 1858 the following notice appeared in the Reading Mercury.

Mr Wm. Jones Williams has been instructed by Mr Thomas Church, who is about to leave, to sell by auction for him his very useful household furniture and drapery stock...

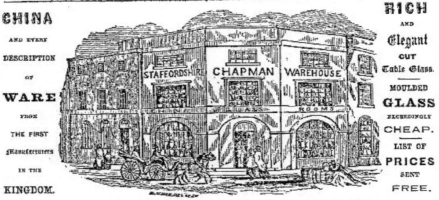

Advert from the Post Office directory for Wiltshire 1855.

Devizes

In 1842 Joseph Chapman had taken over his family's china and glass business on the death of his father Stephen, who had started it in about 1828. His store at Chapel Corner, Devizes was advertised as including a large underground warehouse and separately, a china showroom and a glass showroom. If his advertisements are to be believed, this was a sizeable business. In 1854 he advertised to celebrate the Great Exhibition. On offer was tableware by Minton, awarded the first-class medal at the exhibition.

Perhaps though, things were not going as well as they appeared. After he sold the business to Thomas Church there was a notice of bankruptcy for Joseph Chapman china dealer in Llanelli in 1860 and another in Scarborough in 1862. It's hard to believe that there were three Joseph Chapman china dealers.

On Thursday 28th October 1858 the following notice was placed in the Devizes and Wiltshire Gazette

Joseph Chapman

Begs to tender his grateful thanks for the uniform support he has received for so many years in the china and glass trade and solicits a continuance of the same in favour of his successor, Mr Church. Chapel Corner, Devizes, 20th Oct. 1858.

And immediately underneath

Thomas Church

Having succeeded to the business of Mr Joseph Chapman, hopes by a well selected assortment of china and glass from first rate houses, combined with moderate prices, to merit a continuance of the favours so liberally bestowed on his predecessor.

Thomas Church (in the top hat) outside his shop in Devizes.

Devizes is about 40 miles from East Ilsley. In 1861 it had a population of 6,700 and was the largest town in North Wiltshire. Thomas must have seen the purchase of this china and glass business as a chance for him and his family to move on from the restrictions of village life to the opportunities of a market town. The town would have seemed like a metropolis in comparison with their home village.

Chapel Corner, 16 Maryport St, still stands today. In the 1861 census Thomas and Elizabeth's eldest son William, who was now 15, was an assistant in the shop while his other three children, Wesley, Agnes and Harriet were still at school. Thomas continued to place adverts in a very similar style and often identical words to Joseph Chapman's, particularly in local commercial directories. He advertised repeatedly in the annual Gillman's directory for Devizes taking a full page in addition to his commercial listing. He wasn't the only china and glass dealer in the town. The 1867 Kelly's directory lists three others, but he seems to be the only one who invested heavily in trade directory advertisements.

C. Gillman's Advertising Sheet.

China and Glass Rooms,

16, MARYPORT STREET,

DEVIZES.

THOMAS CHURCH

TENDERS his sincere thanks to his numerous patrons throughout the county for their liberal favors, and begs to assure them it will be his constant study to select the Newest Patterns, of the Best Quality, and offer them at such moderate prices as he trusts will deserve a continuance of their support. He invites the public generally to inspect his immense stock of

USEFUL AND ORNAMENTAL GOODS,

IN

CHINA, GLASS, & WARE.

The large underground WAREHOUSE is well stored with useful articles in Yellow Ware, improved Stone Ware, Chesterfield Ware, Bristol Red Ware, Dorset Brown Ware, Rockingham Ware, Sunderland Ware (well glazed), Measure Mugs and Jugs, Tobacco-pipes, &c.

The SHOP is filled with all kinds of goods in Willow, Rhine, and other patterns of Table Ware, Cream-color Ware, Tea and Breakfast Ware, Toilet Ware, Jugs, Mugs, Teapots (metal tops). China Tea Services from 8s. 6d. per set, Glass Tumblers (pressed) from 3s. per dozen, Goblets, Measures and Ales for taverns, Wines (cut) from 4s. per doz., Salts, Caraffs—with thousands of articles too numerous to particularize.

The CHINA SHOW ROOM contains a choice and large variety of Tea and Breakfast Services, Jugs, Dinner Services, Dessert Sets, handsome Services for Bedrooms, complete.

The GLASS SHOW ROOM is arranged in order with Cut and Engraved Wines, from 7s. to 21s. per dozen; Tumblers, from 7s. to 24s.; Custard Cups, Decanters of all shapes, from 4s. to 50s. per pair; Cut and Pressed Dishes, oval, round, and square; with every requisite in Crystal Cut Table Glass.

A splendid choice of

FANCY & ELEGANT ORNAMENTS

From France, Germany, and Belgium,

Such as figures, Vases, Lustres, Bottles, &c.,

In Gilded China, Glass, and Alabaster.

Oval Paper TRAYS, neat Gold Borders, from One to Three Guineas the Set.

N.B.—Large and small Parties supplied with every description of Goods on HIRE at a moderate charge.

PLATED KNIVES AND FORKS ON SALE OR HIRE.

Thomas Church's advertisement in a local trade directory 1862

Thomas Church's business ambitions didn't stop at Devizes. The Kelly's directory of 1867 records that he also opened a shop in Calne, about seven miles from Devizes, run from 1868 by his eldest son William. William Church was not in the china and glass trade for long. He took up photography and moved to Wootton Bassett, describing himself as 'under the patronage' of the local landowners, the Marquis and Marchioness of Lansdowne. His promising career in photography was cut short by his early death in the 1870s.

There is no way of knowing how well business in Devizes was going for Thomas. We have no accounts, no reminiscences, just what we can glean from press reports and trade directories. So, out of the blue, on January 14th, 1869 comes a notice in the Devizes and Wiltshire Gazette.

Important to Hotel Keepers, Persons Furnishing and Others
China Glass and Staffordshire Warehouse
16 Maryport St. Devizes

Mr J.A. Randall is instructed by Mr T Church, who is leaving Devizes, to sell by auction on the premises on Wednesday, Thursday and Friday January 27th, 28th and 29th, 1869 the remaining portion of his extensive stock in trade of cut, crystal, and other table glass of all descriptions; china and other dinner, dessert, tea and coffee services, water and other jugs, toilette services in great variety; filters, lustres, vases, figures and ornaments, shades, baths, papier mache, and other trays, steel cutlery, plated spoons and forks, candlesticks, and a large collection of useful articles incident to the business.

Also a few lots of household furniture, including chests of drawers, tables and stands, glasses, bureau, grand pianoforte, 8-day clock and other articles.

Catalogues of the whole 3d each (to be returned to purchasers) will be ready and may be obtained at the place of sale, or of the auctioneer, on and after the 23rd instant.

On view, by catalogues only, on Tuesday 26th, from 10am to 6pm. Sale to commence at 12 o'clock each day.

On March 4th in the same paper, Thomas Church thanked his customers and announced that he had disposed of the business to Mr W. Mayers, who already had a business in the town. With that he was gone.

Bridport and Yeovil

Thomas moved to Bridport in Dorset, where he was to be found in the 1871 census with his wife and two remaining unmarried children. Bridport is a small market town a couple of miles inland from the coast at Lyme Bay. As with his other moves, what brought him here is unknown. His stay was only four years, the only advertisement to be found is in the Bridport News on 25th April 1873, announcing that he was moving on.

He either didn't sell all his stock, or he very rapidly bought some more, because six months later he was announcing in the Western Gazette, on 12th September 1873, his arrival in Yeovil.

Important Notice!
To the nobility and gentry and the inhabitants of Yeovil and its vicinity generally.
T. Church, having removed from Bridport to Middle St. Yeovil, has by him a very large surplus stock of China, glass and earthenware which he is offering at an immense reduction.
Dinner sets, dessert sets, tea sets and toilet sets, decanters, wine glasses, tumblers, water bottles etc. richly cut and in great variety.
Also several articles in surplus furniture, great bargains.

*A very large plate glass mahogany frame show stand, with sliding
doors, suitable for a confectioner or chemist for sale.
Note the address.
T. Church
Opposite the George Inn
Middle St. Yeovil*

It is hard to believe that his stay was ever meant to last long, just one
month later he was on the move again. With such an itinerant record,
perhaps he didn't expect to stay in the next town for many years.

CHAPTER TWO

PARADE HOUSE

NORTHAMPTON BOASTS THE LARGEST MARKET SQUARE IN England. The town best known throughout the world for its boots and shoes grew as an important market town, reflecting its position as the hub of trading routes in the heart of England. In 1871 the town's population was 41,000, and there were 4,641 men over the age of twenty working in shoemaking, mostly from home and in small workshops. The establishment of large boot and shoe factories was to come later.

The Market Square, also known as Market Hill, was the hub of the town's commercial life. In 1873 a large property at the top of the hill, in the middle of the north side of the square, was available for occupation. Its prominent site made it the perfect spot for a shopkeeper.

There were some big changes on the Market Square, reflected in three advertisements carried by the Northampton Mercury of 27th December 1873. In the first, the Borough Council announced the opening of 'A New General Market' on the square with stalls to be let for one year by an auction to be held on 29th December. The second offered a property for sale, pointing out *"The Corporation having ordered the removal of all markets from their present sites* to the Market Square materially enhances the value of all property surrounding it, and consequently, these premises offer a most desirable opportunity to any person desirous of possessing a really valuable property". However, Thomas Church had already got the premises he wanted. The smallest of these three adverts, headed 'The Parade House Glass and China Rooms Northampton', announced his arrival to 'the house lately in the occupation of Mr Franklin, called "Leamington House".

Thomas took over the property from a wine merchant. As a supporter of the temperance movement he may have found that particularly ironic, but Mr Franklin had not gone out of business. He moved to Guildhall Rd where he continued to trade for many years and became a hotelier. He is best remembered today for giving his name to Franklins Gardens, the home of Northampton Saints Rugby Club.

Northampton has traditionally been a strongly anti-establishment town. Never popular with royalty, the establishment of a university here was curtailed in the 13th century due to the students displeasing the king. The town took Cromwell's side in the Civil War, and when Charles II came to the throne, he had the town walls torn down.

The Church family's non-conformist faith fitted well with Northampton. Thomas initially joined the Methodist church in Gold St, but later switched to the long-established Baptist church in College St. Perhaps Thomas already had business interests in Northampton. An advertisement of 1867 refers to 'D. Church, berlin wool and fancy repository' at 50a the Drapery. There is a small advert in the Northampton Mercury in 1869 for a 'governess agency and servants registry office, conducted by Mr Church, Berlin and Fancy Repository at 12 Parade Northampton', just two doors from Parade house. A year later this business was sold. Maybe it is just a coincidence that two decades later Thomas went on to run a servants' registry in Reading before he died in 1892.

Wilfrid Church, in his short history of Church's China, links the berlin wool business to the family. There is no evidence of anyone related to Thomas living in Northampton before his arrival, but with his known business activities in several other towns, it is possible that he did have some prior interest in the town. Without any other firm evidence, there is nothing but the availability of a large shop in a prime position to explain the family's move to Northampton.

Thomas Church's Shop in Parade House, before 1881.

Reading the Riot Act

Charles Bradlaugh was a man with a colossal national reputation. Loved and loathed in equal measure for his atheism, republicanism and radical politics, he championed universal suffrage, trade unions, Irish home rule and the rights of the people of India. He had founded the National Secular Society, had been involved in numerous legal disputes over his championing of birth control and had toured the country as a noted lecturer and publisher.

He wasn't born in Northampton and had never lived in the town, but he had chosen Northampton to pursue his political career, so far without success. He first stood for election in 1868, splitting the Liberal vote and coming fifth.

Northampton, like many County Boroughs at that time, elected two MP's to represent one constituency. When the Church family arrived both MP's were Liberal, Charles Gilpin and Lord Henley. A general election was due at any time. Bradlaugh had once again been refused the Liberal nomination but was regularly in Northampton campaigning. The new year would prove a turbulent year in Northampton politics, one that would directly impact upon the Church family.

On 24th January 1874 Gladstone dissolved parliament for the country's first general election requiring the use of the secret ballot. Charles Bradlaugh was on a lecture tour of America at the time. His nomination was submitted in his absence and a vigorous campaign was run by his supporters. His daughter wrote that his campaign song written for the previous election "Bradlaugh for Northampton" was heard throughout the streets at all hours of the day. The result was a Liberal loss; Pickering Phipps, one of the Conservative candidates topped the poll with 2,690 votes, the Liberal, Charles Gilpin was also elected with 2,310. The second Conservative and Liberal candidates came third and fourth and Charles Bradlaugh came last, but with a respectable 1,653 votes.

Thomas Church was to learn that living on Northampton's Market Square meant he would never miss a big event. On 10th February the defeated candidate arrived back from America. Bradlaugh's daughter wrote: -

"The scene at the station defied description, and the crowd assembled to meet him extended right into the town. Along the route to the Market Square people were at the windows, and

even upon the housetops, anxious to see and greet the defeated candidate. He addressed a few words to the mass of people gathered in the square...".

Five thousand people heard him speak that evening, almost as many as the total number of people who had voted, but most of the men and all the women still did not have the vote. Thomas had only been in the town for two months; this must have been an extraordinary spectacle for him and his young family.

The health of Charles Gilpin was poor and there was talk of his early retirement. Bradlaugh once again suggested a ballot to choose the Liberal candidate but the idea was rejected. He was planning another lecture tour in the States, but Gilpin unexpectedly died in September. A by-election was called and Bradlaugh cancelled his trip. This time William Fowler was the official Liberal candidate and Charles Merewether was chosen for the Conservatives. The campaign was vicious, with personal insults hurled at Bradlaugh by Fowler, including accusations that he was unmarried, his children therefore bastards and his mother dependent on poor relief (actually she was dead). Bradlaugh hit back at Fowler calling him a liar and a coward, which only lead to more abuse being hurled on him, particularly by the Mercury newspaper, whose offices were next door to Thomas Church's shop.

The result was declared on October 6th, and it brought disappointment once again. Merewether gained the seat for the Conservatives with 2,171 votes, Fowler 1,836 and Bradlaugh 1,766. It was a close three way marginal, the Conservative winning on the split Liberal vote.

This time tempers overflowed. A riot started outside Fowler's headquarters at The Palmerston Inn on the east side of the Market Square. Bradlaugh succeeded in dispersing the crowd before he left the town to catch his ship for America. With their leader gone, the riot resumed and spread from The Palmerston Inn to the offices of the Northampton Mercury, the paper which had supported Fowler's campaign. Thomas Church didn't just occupy the shop next door; his family home upstairs stretched above the Mercury office.

The army was called, and the Riot Act was read. Cobblestones were torn off the square and hurled through windows. The Riot Act was read a second time. Inevitably, it was not just the newspaper offices that suffered, but the upstairs windows of Parade House too. The riot attracted nationwide attention in the newspapers, with one report that both Liberal and Conservative tradesmen had suffered significantly from damage to their property.

A few weeks later a special session of the magistrates' court was held to determine damages claimed by several town centre residents and businesses. The Mayor, W. Adkins, chaired the magistrates' bench and Mr Shoosmith, the Town Clerk, represented the council, who were liable to pay claims from the borough rate. According to the Northampton Mercury, claims for damages were under an Act of Parliament passed some years earlier. This stated that *'any house or other property should be feloniously demolished, pulled down, or destroyed, wholly or in part, by any persons, riotously or tumultuously assembled together, in every such case every inhabitant of the borough should be liable therefor.'*

First, the court heard the claim by the landlord of the Palmerston Inn and the town clerk accepted it without challenge.

Thomas Church's claim for £8 10s came next, but his claim was more complicated. The target of the attack was the Mercury premises, not Thomas Church's home and shop. Mr Hensman, acting on Thomas Church's behalf, said that *'a most determined attack was made on the Mercury premises and upon his client's premises, which in the eyes of the multitude were supposed to be one and the same building.... Several attacks were made, but the chief one was just before ten o'clock, and would undoubtedly have ended in the mob getting into both houses had not the military arrived on the scene'.* The Mercury reported Thomas Church's evidence to the court as follows.

"A gentleman came to the door in great haste and told him the mob were smashing the Lord Palmerston and were coming to smash The Mercury. He immediately went indoors, drew the shutters and made as much preparation as possible. Soon afterwards, and several times during the evening up to ten o'clock, stones started coming through the windows, damaging the furniture in the room, completely smashing a large pier glass [a wall mirror], knocking ornaments off the bedroom shelves, and destroying the whole of the glass in the bow and other windows. Just before ten o'clock the attack was the hottest, and he was afraid that they would effect an entrance. The arrival of the military caused them to disperse, and after a time all was quiet. The next morning, he picked up 108 large stones in his rooms. He believed the damage he sustained was in consequence of an impression that the premises belonged to the Mercury office; two of the windows were over the office."

The Town Clerk challenged the claim that the crowd mistook Thomas Church's home for the Mercury office *"Everyone was aware that Mr Church's premises were not the Mercury and the crowd knew it perfectly well. Therefore, although he did not wish to put any obstacle in the way of the sufferers obtaining compensation, he must urge that it would not be legal to grant the claim made in this case."*

Another witness called heard a voice in the crowd shout that it *'was all the same'*, and therefore, because the crowd confused Thomas Church's property with the Mercury office, it was argued that his claim was legitimate. The magistrates found in favour of Thomas Church and granted his claim with costs.

A grainy picture shows the Mercury Printing Office with its smashed windows, and in front of it a riotous crowd, police with truncheons in the air, and to the left the shuttered shop widows of Thomas Church's shop.

The Bradlaugh Riots. Thomas Church's shop on the left, The Mercury on the right.

Charles Bradlaugh was eventually rewarded for his efforts, being elected Liberal MP for Northampton in 1880. He went on to face the battle for which he is most remembered today, to win his right as an atheist to take his seat in Parliament. He continued to be re-elected until The House of Commons finally accepted that he could take his seat after taking a non-religious oath that is still used today. He died, still serving as Northampton's MP, in 1891.

The Spencer family

Thomas and Elizabeth brought their two remaining unmarried children with them to Northampton. In 1877 the 23-year-old Wesley Thomas Church married Sarah Spencer. She came from a typical Northampton family. Her father William was a self-employed shoemaker, living and working in St Giles St in the heart of the town. Her grandfather John, who had died a few years earlier at the age of 91, was also a shoemaker. He was born in Kislingbury, coming into town to work in Gas St.

John Spencer handed down one chilling artefact to his descendants. It was a pair of handcuffs he had used as a constable in the 1820's. They had been used to constrain George Catherall, better known as 'Captain Slash', the head of a gang of thieves who terrorised local fairs. In 1826 they attacked Boughton Fair, an important event held a few miles north of Northampton. Things did not go to plan for Captain Slash. The fair's stallholders fought back, his gang were driven off, many were arrested and carted off to Northampton Gaol. Their ringleader's skull was broken, but when a bystander suggested he was dead, he roused himself saying 'I am not dead and shan't be until I have a rope round my neck'. He was handcuffed to John Spencer and taken to Northampton Gaol.

Captain Slash was sentenced to death, but he made one last gesture of defiance before he died. His mother had told him many years before that he would 'die with his shoes on', a term used to describe a violent end. To prove her wrong, as he was led to the gallows, he kicked his shoes into the crowd.

The Northampton Directory of 1853 published by Thomas Phillips lists William Spencer of St. Giles St and his father John, now in Green St., as two out of 49 shoemakers in the town as distinct from 69 shoe *manufacturers*. It seems that the Spencers had become self-employed craftsmen rather than working for or employing others.

Sarah's mother was born in Abington, a couple of miles east of Northampton, where her father, Joseph Moore, was a farm labourer on the Abington estate, popular now as Abington Park.

Wesley moved out of Parade House and set up home with his new wife in a small terraced house, 10 Thenford St, recently built as the town expanded outside the historic boundary marked by the line of the demolished town wall. By the time of the 1881 census Sarah's elderly parents had retired and joined them there. Their first child William Wesley was born in Thenford St on 15th March 1880.

Changes at Parade House

For some years Thomas Church had allowed a room in Parade House to be used for a dental surgery. The following notice appeared in the Northampton Mercury on January 27th 1877.

"If you want to ensure perfect mastication, and to enjoy your meals, there are certainly no Artificial Teeth for ease and comfort so perfect as those recently patented by Messrs Lewis Mosely and Son, 448 Strand, opposite Charing Cross Railway Station, and 30 Berners St., Oxford St. Between these artificial teeth and the natural organs there is no difference whatever, while for natural appearance, the restoration of youthful features, they are unrivalled. The charges are so moderate as to be within the reach of all. ... Attendance at Parade House, Market Square, Northampton every Friday and Saturday. Consultation free, Established upwards of 50 years."

Mr Mosely's name was being used in adverts for dentistry elsewhere. He probably did visit the town, there is an advert for a Mr Mosely holding a dental surgery in Northampton in 1842, but it is unlikely that it was he who was practising in Parade House. On 11th May 1881 Messrs W.P and E. Sherwood of Parade House described themselves as successors to Lewis Mosely. Thomas and Elizabeth Church's remaining unmarried daughter Harriet Anne Jemima (variously called Harriet or Annie) was living with them in Parade House. She soon got to know the young dentist and on 29th August she and William Sherwood were married, not in Northampton, but for an unknown reason in Battersea.

In March and April, in a succession of adverts, Thomas Church announced that he was selling off his entire stock 'in consequence of alteration to premises'. Looking at photographs it appears that an additional shop window was placed on the left-hand side of the building, presumably with internal alterations to expand the shop. William Sherwood (together with E. Sherwood) moved their dental practice out of Parade House to 63 Marefair, where he lived with his new wife. Wesley moved from Thenford St. back into Parade House with his wife, baby son and elderly in-laws. Another child was on the way and on 1st June 1882 Wilfrid Spencer Church was born in Parade House.

For a brief period, the china business was known as Church & Son. In September 1881 a new shop was acquired in the Drapery, where the stock of Mr G. Cooper had been purchased for sale. The following year on 8th May 1882 a long advert was placed in the Chronicle and Echo by Dr. Siemms, a visiting chiropodist who was working from Church's China at 21 The Drapery offering his cure for corns.

The partnership of Church and Son was soon over. Early in 1882 advertisements appeared under the name of W.T. Church, referring to the 'long established' business. It had only been in town for nine years and in the ownership of the family for just 24 years.

A notice on 8th March 1884 in the Chronicle and Echo said that 21 The Drapery was now let, *'The whole of the stock must be sold in a few weeks. If you want a bargain in china, glass and earthenware come at once.'* A couple of weeks later the Northampton Mercury reported that Thomas Church, earthenware dealer, 21 The Drapery, had been summoned to a petty court session for allowing his chimney to catch fire through his own neglect. He was fined 1 shilling and 9 shillings costs. Around this time Thomas and Elizabeth left Northampton, leaving their son Wesley and daughter Harriet and their young families behind.

In an advert on August 16th, 1884 W.T. Church pointed out *'he has only one china and glass establishment in the town and that is the old established shop at No 10 the Parade, Market Square.'* With his father gone and the shop in the Drapery closed, he clearly wanted to make it known that he alone was now in charge.

There was one more change to the shop the following year. On August 8th, 1885 a notice appeared in the Northampton Mercury advertising *'shop only to let. W.T. Church, having taken the next shop will shortly have for disposal his present one. New plate glass front. Best position in the town. – Apply at 10 The Parade Market Square Northampton.'* He must have changed his mind, but he did re-fit the shop. In October a series of adverts appeared stating *'W.T. Church, having fitted up his new shop begs to invite inspection. The whole of his showroom and warehouse, which are well stocked with the newest designs in Wedgewood and Minton China, are now open to the public.'* The pedant will notice the common misspelling of Wedgwood (there should be only one 'e') but the more serious error is the failure to include any address. However, in another notice he advertised for new staff at The Parade, Market Square.

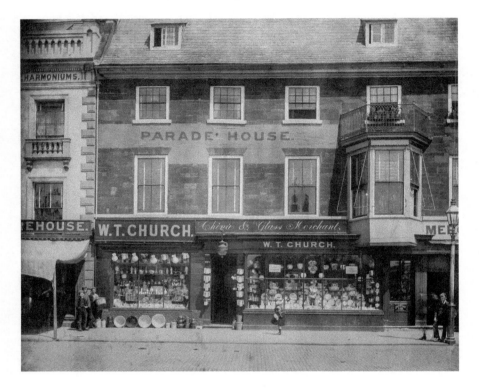

W.T. Church's expanded shop in Parade House, after 1881.

Life in Parade House

Wilfrid Church's early memories, recalled as an old man over eighty years later, give a colourful insight into life on the Market Square in the final decades of the nineteenth century.

Writing about Parade House he remembered:

'The rooms in these old premises were large and spread out as would be expected of one of the old Victorian Hostels. The different floors were approached by a balustraded and wide staircase which

reached up to the top storey; from this elevation you could look down a kind of square well to the ground floor. The ground levels were occupied by our showrooms and general stock, except for a capacious kitchen and a terrifying 'coal hole'. This culinary department was stone flagged and was a happy playground for cockroaches. The beetle trap was constantly in requisition and a kettle of boiling water was served out to them in the mornings.

'*There were numerous bedrooms and two particularly fine sitting rooms, in one of which an oil painting was permanently fixed over the fireplace. This can now be seen in Abington Park Museum.*

'*The windows on the first floor, looking out onto the Market Square could be shuttered. The outlook from here provided us with much interest and entertainment. The rooms at the rear of the building had something of a haunted atmosphere about them, and we as children had fanciful thoughts of ghastly apparitions gliding along these creaky-floored rooms. There was a damp and unwholesome cellar approached by stone steps as to a dungeon.*'

He wrote too about the Market Square.

'*In my early days the Market Square would at certain times be brightened up garishly and made to resound with discordancy by the arrival of a "fair." There were round-a-bouts, boxing booth, snap dragon confections &c. The glare and tumult persisted until about 11pm, when the bellowing organ gave as its lullaby "Christians Awake".*

'*About the first week in June, wagons of wool would arrive drawn by sturdy horses. These were from the outlying farms and soon uploaded, weighed and bid for. This was indeed a noteworthy sight.*

'*The cheese fair was also an attraction, when the large cylindrical blocks were brought for sale from many parts. A gauge like knife could be inserted for the prospective buyer to judge whether the commodity was to his taste or not.*

A trader from Kislingbury on the Market Square in about 1887. The picture was claimed to be the first in Northampton taken with a hand-held camera.

'On one occasion a menagerie (Wombwell's) arrived on the square, the roar of wild beasts sounding somewhat fearsome during the night.

'There was certainly plenty of interest continually taking place, this being the town's centre. There were the politicians holding forth from the steps of the fountain sometimes being baptised by little urchins who had climbed up above and flipped water from the ornamental cupolas. Persons incapable through drink being bustled across the square by the police to the Dychurch Lane Police Station, the youthful followers would then stand and loudly deride as the unfortunate inebriates disappeared.

'At certain times the volunteer regiment would arrive headed by the band where it was then dismissed. Colonel Hollis, who had an outfitters shop at the corner of the Parade was, I believe, the officer in charge. Also, there were the usual celebrations, processions, &c. The twice weekly markets must be mentioned *where stalls and open spaces were occupied by bona fide country vendors who would arrive by cart. Saturday was the busiest day but Wednesday had but a few stalls in evidence.'*

Having the local newspaper next door was a constant irritation.

'There was a passage flanking our shop, down which when the editions of the Mercury were released, a stampede of many hurrying youths would emerge and pour forth in all directions into the Market Square, As the partition was a flimsy one there was quite a rattle of china and glass during this minor earthquake. Of a more romantic nature one of our shop entrances was very near an adjoining exit of the Mercury Office. As our assistants were mainly of the gentler sex, they would sometimes attract the youthful reporters of the offices next door. These young men might of course have been mistaken for prospective customers whereas there was more of Romeo and Juliet in this connection. One of these reporters, a Mr Saunders, left the town and took up a high journalistic position, leaving behind a little china shepherdess.'

Complaints about boys hanging around the Mercury Offices were taken up before Wilfrid was born. At a meeting of the Borough Petty Sessions on June 4th 1880, chaired by the Mayor Joseph Gurney, Thomas Church and neighbour Mr Hall made a complaint about the newspaper's proprietor. He said his doorway was close to the doorway of the Mercury office, where during the latter part of the evening there were from three to four score of boys blocking up the pavement causing an obstruction to the foot passengers. It wasn't just the Mercury that was being criticised, also 'the Guardian' of Gold St was subject to complaints from its neighbours. After a debate among the magistrates the Mayor summed up *"the attention of the police and of the proprietors of the papers having been called to this matter, I have no doubt that the nuisance will be remedied."*

The nuisance clearly was not remedied. The following year on March 30th Fanny Richardson, William Starmer, Edwin Jones and Harry Whitney were before the magistrates charged with 'obstructing the passengers on the parade by loitering on the same'. Police Constable Green said that the previous Tuesday at a quarter to six he saw from 70 to 80 boys around four or five women, who were delivering papers on the footway. The Chief Constable cross examined several witnesses including Mr Hall and Wesley Church who said he saw the Police Constable caution the woman that it was illegal to sell newspapers on the pavement, the PC kept boys away. Mrs Richardson was fined 2s 6d. Mr Dicey of the newspaper said that he was seeking to make arrangements with his neighbour Mr Church to resolve the nuisance. The Mayor said that the boys should be at school and they were only fined costs.

Church's China was not just a retail business. It offered china and glass for hire, and a packing service. When wealthy people travelled, they took their fine china with them, and W.T. Church was employed to pack their china and glass for the journey. Wilfrid recalled one such packing trip, he thought in 1893, when he would have been eleven.

'At certain times of the year the Marquis of Northampton would visit Exmoor on a stag hunting expedition taking with him a fairly large retinue. At such times my father would be requisitioned to visit Castle Ashby to pack up china and glass for their safe conveyance to the hunting grounds. There in the large servants' hall in the castle I can remember joining in the lunch with the large number of servants and general staff, the baker, the butler, the housekeeper, the coachman &c. After this repast I was taken across the snow covered park to see Knuckle Bone Arbour, a bower of retreat, the floor of which was laid with the knuckle bones of deer.'

Wesley Thomas Church

W.T. Church is the first member of the family for whom it is possible to build a reasonably complete pen portrait, partly from the writings of his son, but also from various other sources. Wilfrid summed him up. *'As a Nonconformist, a Liberal and a staunch teetotaller, my parent was of course very much in the minority. He retained a sociable disposition and in spite of his strong convictions was widely respected.'* He was hardly in a minority in the first two. Northampton returned Liberal MP's for most of Wesley's life and retained a powerful non-conformist tradition. Perhaps Wilfrid meant that in the middle-class environment in which Wesley circulated, he was in a minority.

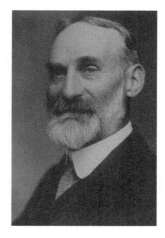

WT Church

Wesley switched from the Methodist tradition of his father and grandfather to College St. Baptist Church. Wilfrid described him as having 'advanced opinions', holding to a personal prayer 'Make me neither rich nor poor'.

He took up the cause of the temperance movement with enthusiasm. In 1887 he presided at an open-air meeting of the Temperance Mission on the Market Square. He became a shareholder of Northampton Temperance Hall, built to provide social facilities without alcohol.

He was a member of a society formed to promote abstinence from alcohol called the Independent Order of Rechabites. Named after an ancient Arabic tribe, the Rechabites organised themselves in a way which looks masonic. The lodges were called tents, and there were three degrees of membership: The Knight of Temperance, The Knight of Fortitude and the Covenanted Knight of Fortitude.

Related to the Rechabites was the Independent Order of Good Templars, that campaigned for prohibition of alcohol and sought to provide alcohol free social facilities for young people. The Northampton Mercury in 1898 reported that a meeting of the William Carey Lodge of Good Templars at College St. Schools was chaired by Bro. W.T. Church and the pianist was Mrs. W.T. Church.

He had a range of interests outside business; foremost of those was chess. The first record of this was in 1884, when the Northampton

Mercury reported that W.T. Church had been appointed to the committee of the St. Giles Young Men's Chess Club. In a couple of years, the 'Young Men' were removed from the name of the club, and in 1889 he was appointed to a sub-committee of Northamptonshire Chess Club to help them find new rooms for their matches. He contributed in a whole range of roles, to Northamptonshire and later Northampton Chess Club, for the rest of his life, becoming eventually an honorary life member.

Wesley Church had an allotment at Cliftonville, on the edge of the town, but not just for gardening. William Blumson, who had an adjoining allotment would, according to Wilfrid, '*join at an al fresco game while the weeds grew up all around.*' Chess also took over at the shop, a Rev. Sams used to call '*when chess men would be brought out and placed on a bench in the back warehouse. Here they could be found poring over pawns, kings &c while the dust floated all around.*'

Cycling was an important and fashionable pastime for keeping fit. Wilfrid says that his father was one of the first people in Northampton to ride a cycle with pneumatic tyres. He cycled into the country with friends on a Thursday afternoon (early closing day in Northampton) and bank holidays. One such friend was A.E. Towers, a gentleman's outfitter, who unlike W.T. Church was a church going Tory. According to Wilfrid '*these two gentlemen would embark on these outings quite happily but had been known to make the return journey individually and some distance apart.*'

W.T. Church's friends included the architect Matthew Holding. He designed St. Matthews Church, then on the edge of town, noted for its tall spire. This was largely financed by a wealthy local brewer named Phipps. The spire became known locally as 'Phipps's fire escape', as it ensured his admittance to heaven.

Wilfrid described Holding as a most interesting man with a quiet and subtle humour. In 1889 Wesley commissioned some china to commemorate Holding's new Guildhall extension. Only one plate is known to survive. Other friends included the Rev. Archibald Wake of

Courteenhall and Mr Wren, whose name is remembered from the lids of the shoe polish tins.

Wesley and Sarah Church enjoyed music. Wilfrid refers to performances with the Rev. and Mrs P.H. Smith, (the minister of College St. Chapel and his wife) of "O, that we two were maying" and "Madam will you walk?" with his mother accompanying on the piano. His parents were actively involved in schools linked to College St. Baptist chapel. According to an article in the Northampton Mercury in 1895

Sarah Church

Wesley reported to an annual meeting of parents, teachers and old pupils of the College St chapel Sunday School.

W.T. Church was a keen proponent of homeopathy. Wilfrid recalls:

'Dr. Wilkinson, who lived in Newland was our medical practitioner and would, if occasion so required, drive up in pony and trap, wearing a top hat and looking quite handsome and amiable with his trimmed side whiskers. Sometimes it was Dr Clifton who prescribed the little pills, aconite, belladonna &c for our indispositions. Mr Cowdery, a chemist at the corner of the entrance to Corn Exchange, kept a wide range of these rather harmless medicines.'

A generation moves on

Within the space of nine years, between 1886 and 1895, a generation of the family were gone. William and Sarah Spencer had moved to Parade House with their daughter and son in law. William died there in 1887 at the age of 74 and Sarah in 1895 at the age of 79. Wesley's parents had moved away to London, and he probably saw little of them, Wilfrid had no recollection of his grandfather. In 1886 the family received the news of Elizabeth's death in Bayswater in London. Four years later Thomas died in Reading at the age of 69. The notice of his death in the Northampton Mercury on July 25th, 1890 tells us that it was due to an unexpected stroke. '*He was known as an ardent temperance reformer. A man of quiet and unostentatious habit, he was respected by a large circle for his sturdy adherence to principle.*' His probate record showed that he left £269 4s 9d, and that he had kept a boarding house in Bayswater but had moved to Minster St. in Reading as a 'Keeper of Servants Registry'. It is sad to think that he died away from his family. There are hints in the tone of the adverts in 1883-4 that he did not see eye to eye with Wesley. It's possible too that he was unhappy with his daughter's marriage to William Sherwood. That's just speculation, but as we shall see, he may have had good reason to be worried for his daughter.

The Sherwood Family tragedy

Until an 1878 act of Parliament, anyone could practise as a dentist. From then on, the use of the term 'dentist' or 'dental surgeon' was restricted to qualified and registered practitioners. William Sherwood described himself as a 'surgeon dentist'. He advertised regularly, the following from February 26th 1885 is typical.

PAINLESS DENTISTRY
Messrs. W.P. & E. Sherwood, surgeon dentists
63 Marefair (near Castle Station) Northampton
Messrs Sherwood's improved artificial teeth are recommended by most eminent of the medical profession as undoubtedly the best substitutes for the natural organs, being fixed without extracting the old stumps of teeth or any painful operation whatever. They are unrivalled for durability, comfort and life like appearances and when placed in the mouth defy detection by the closest observer.

Messrs Sherwood's speciality is the use of Nitrogen Oxide gas, Ether calorific fluid &c enables them to guarantee all operations appertaining to dentistry perfectly painless.

Single teeth from 5s.; sets from 4 to 25 guineas. Consultation and every information free.

63 Marefair Northampton

William Sherwood didn't just work from home. He advertised weekly surgeries in Wolverton, Thrapston, Oundle and elsewhere, and presumably he had plenty of work. He and Harriet soon started a family. Edward Sherwood was born in 1882, Ivy the following year and William in 1886.

In 1891 there was some shocking news. The Northampton Mercury on Friday February 20th reported that William Sherwood was summoned before Northampton Petty Sessions, chaired by the Mayor, on a charge of indecently assaulting one Annie Jolley. *'The complainant stated that the defendant had assaulted her on the morning in question and on several occasions. In cross examination she said the defendant had been drinking heavily lately and did not know what he was doing. He had been very strange in his way for some time, and on some occasions had done things that she believed he did not know what he was actually doing. The bench dismissed the case.'*

Today it appears astonishing that the case was dismissed, there is no suggestion of any challenge to the charge and the victim reported that it was a repeated offence.

William Sherwood continued with his dentistry and early in 1893 learned that after a gap of seven years his wife was pregnant once again. She gave birth. but developed pleuro-pneumonia and died on 26th December.

Harriet's death left William with four young children to support. He had the income to employ a servant, so difficult though this was, it should not have been as hard as for many people with a smaller income, but he had a record of drink and mental health problems.

William continued to advertise his dental work, with weekly visits to Oundle and Market Harborough.

On October 30th 1894, the following news was reported in the Northampton Chronicle & Echo.

'Shocking affair at Berrywood Asylum
'Supposed suicide of Mr. W.P. Sherwood

'A painful sensation was caused throughout the town this morning when the rumour gained currency that Mr. William Peter Sherwood, the well-known dentist of Marefair had committed suicide. The report unhappily turned out to be correct. Mr Sherwood, who was 40 years of age, had for some time suffered from mental affliction, and only last Friday afternoon, before a special sitting of the Borough Magistrates... he was brought up on a charge of wandering abroad, and supposed to be a person of unsound mind. Mr Sherwood was ordered to be removed to an asylum, and he was soon after conveyed to Berry Wood. About four o'clock in the morning he was found by an attendant with a strip of sheet fastened around his neck. He was quite dead, and the appearances pointed to suicide by hanging.'

W.T. Church attended the inquest. William John Clayton, one of the witnesses, said that *'the last time he had seen him he was wrong in the mind, necessitating him sitting up with him. He was not at all violent, but he had the delusion that electric wires were all about the place. Witness went for Dr. Stone, but during his absence the deceased left the house and gave himself up at the police station. The police took steps to have him removed to the asylum. Deceased had been unable to attend to his business a fortnight previously owing to his having given way to drink. He had never threatened to destroy himself but had threatened to destroy other people. His wife died last Christmas and there was a family of four children, all under the age of twelve.'*

The inquest went on to report his admission to Berrywood asylum (later St. Crispin's Hospital), when he was 'quite cheerful'. He was seen several times each day and he showed no signs of a suicidal tendency. He had delusions about dynamite *'and there was no doubt of his being insane'*. The newspaper report went on to describe how he was found at four in the morning strangled with a piece of bed sheet attached to the corner of the bed, with his head a few inches above the floor. A verdict of self- inflicted death from strangulation was recorded, exonerating the hospital staff from any blame.

The story that passed down through the family was only that William Sherwood was an alcoholic. Wilfrid Church never reported how he died. What is clear is that William Sherwood was a heavy drinker, but he had mental health problems that may have caused and may have been compounded by the drinking. His death would have confirmed the Church family's abhorrence of drink, and doubtless had a profound impact upon Wesley's four young children, who for a while at least had to share their house with the orphaned Sherwood children.

Wilfrid says that Wesley and Sarah took care for the children, but that was only for a few years. He wrote: *'A pecuniary provision was not attached to the misfortune, the pressure on our family economy was indeed very severe. How my parents faced this predicament it is hard to understand. The household was now a very full one, there being father, mother, two sons, two daughters, four orphans, two 'living in' shop assistants and two maids.'*

By the time of the 1901 census none of the Sherwood children were living with the Church family. Edward, the eldest, was a dental mechanic in Barnstaple, Devon. He served in the first world war and became a dentist in London. He briefly returned to Northampton to visit Wilfrid in the 1940's. Ivy, who was living in London with a relative, married but died in 1922. William was a pupil at the Royal Masonic School in London. His father had been a mason, so the masonic lodge were likely to be assisting with the children's education. Ten years later he was a music hall actor and later went to live in Argentina where he died in 1962. It is not clear what happened to the fourth child.

Holly Road

The end of the 19th century was a period of huge housing growth in Northampton. The town spread eastwards, engulfing the rural parish of Abington, which grew from 143 in 1841 (including Sarah Church's grandparents) to several thousand in 1891. Rows of solidly built Victorian terraces interspersed with new shoe factories housed the town's rapidly expanding population. On the main roads, larger properties, such as those overlooking Northampton Racecourse, were occupied by the burgeoning middle classes, including factory owners and shopkeepers.

Sometime before 1898 W.T. Church joined this exodus from the town centre. He acquired 27 Holly Road, about a mile outside the town centre and built probably about ten years earlier. The new tramline along the Kettering Road gave convenient access to the town centre. Their new home would have brought some peace compared to the noise and activity of the Market Square. It was to remain Wesley and Sarah's home for the rest of their lives.

The growth of the town was bringing other pressures to bear. There was a demand for new and improved shopping facilities in the town centre. Wesley may have been aware of this before the move to Holly Rd, but if not, he very soon would. In 1899 the local newspapers published the first news of a proposal to redevelop the north side of the Market Square. This would require the demolition of Parade House, which had been the home of the family business for 26 years.

CHAPTER THREE

THE DRAB PERIOD

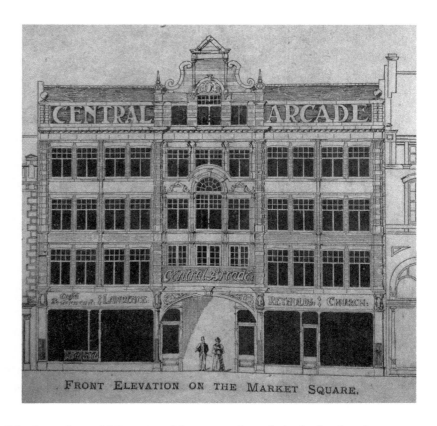

'The Central Arcade' Drawing of the proposed arcade in the developer's prospectus.

Northampton Town Improvements
A Covered Market and Arcade

Improvement and progress are in the air of Northampton, and the rapid strides that are being made by the municipal authorities in street improvements are, as we have pointed out from time to time, being extensively supplemented by the business community of the Borough. New factories, new business houses and new premises of all kinds are springing up, and the commercial future of the Greater Northampton, with its 100,000 population is made all the more potential for prosperity by this ready co-operation of the inhabitants with the Corporation in improvements of our main thoroughfares.

It is with pleasure that we are able to announce the latest movement in this direction. It is only right that our handsome Market Square- one of the finest in the country- should not be omitted from the extensive alterations now being made to advance Northampton's attractiveness. It has been an open secret for some time past that the large site lately occupied by the offices of the 'Northampton Mercury' and the 'Northampton Daily Reporter', and the larger part of which is still in the occupation of Mr. W.T. Church, china merchant, was to be dealt with in a manner which should greatly improve the Market Square. The removal of the Mercury and Daily Reporter to the handsome premises they now occupy left the whole of the old site- running some 400 feet back and comprising over 30,000 square feet-open for the improvement contemplated. This is no other than a commodious and attractive arcade of shops and offices, with warehouse accommodation at the back. ...

Northampton Daily Reporter
November 29th 1899

THE OLD CENTURY ENDED WITH PROMISES OF A BRIGHT, MODERN future for the centre of Northampton. The plans were not just for an arcade of new shops, but for a covered market too. The Northampton Estates and Improvement Corporation (a name that echoes down the 20th century to the Northampton Development Corporation) was formed to undertake the development. A week later it issued a prospectus and invited applications for shares.

7 Sheep St.

Wesley Church probably knew for some time that his shop had to move. Events now proceeded quickly. His son Wilfrid wrote: *'We had notice to quit and so we were placed in some difficulty in obtaining suitable space and accommodation in the centre of the town. We tried many positions all of which did not appear to suit our particular needs. Ultimately, we decided on 7 Sheep Street, belonging to Messrs. Brice and Sons, The Drapery.'*

In the new year advertisements were placed in the local newspapers declaring that W.T. Church had to clear his entire stock, as the premises had been sold. The sale started on February 17th, 1900. The final clearance sale took place in the last week of April and the new shop opened in Sheep St. on 1st May.

Business did not go well in Sheep St. Wilfrid wrote *'We found that position being on the wrong side of a busy thoroughfare was not conducive to business as customers did not wish to cross the road which even in those days was a risky adventure.'* He went on

A leaflet advertising the shop move.

to say '*...I am disinclined to record very much of this somewhat drab period.*'

Royal events are always good for trade in the china business, and 1902 saw the first coronation in the business's history. W.T. Church took advantage of this with advertisements, which probably cheered up this 'drab' period.

The newly passed Shop Hours Act gave local authorities the power to declare an early closing day during the week. In 1904, a public meeting was organised in the Temperance Hall by the National Union of Shop Assistants, Warehousemen and Clerks to urge Northampton Borough Council to use this power. The keynote speech was given by Margaret Bondfield, then assistant general secretary of the Shopworkers Union. Over twenty years later she became Labour MP for Northampton and the first woman cabinet minister. Wesley spoke in support of implementing the act. The meeting decided that a deputation of six people (three shopkeepers and three appointed by the union) should make the case to the town council. W.T. Church was one of the shopkeepers. Thursday became Northampton's early closing day, and Church's China, like many businesses, abided by it right up to the 1970's.

Two advertisements in 1904, and a piece of headed notepaper from the time show that W.T Church briefly opened another shop at 161 Kettering Rd.

Summaries of the business's annual accounts exist from 1906 onwards, the total value of sales in that year were £1,315.

The Emporium Arcade

Parade House was quickly demolished after Wesley moved out, and work started on the exciting new retail development. On June 16th, 1900 the Northampton Daily Reporter carried the following report.

The Northampton Arcade and Covered Market

We are authoritatively informed that the first public work contemplated by the Northampton Estates and Improvement Corporation Limited is now begun. The builders are already at work demolishing the back portion of the old Mercury premises on the Parade. Out of a number of tenders from local builders that of Mr. A.J. Chown of Kingsthorpe has been accepted and the work will be executed with despatch. As our readers will remember, the whole of the vast site until recently occupied by the printing and publishing offices of this journal and the china emporium of Mr. W.T. Church, together with two properties opening directly onto Newland, is embraced in the scheme.

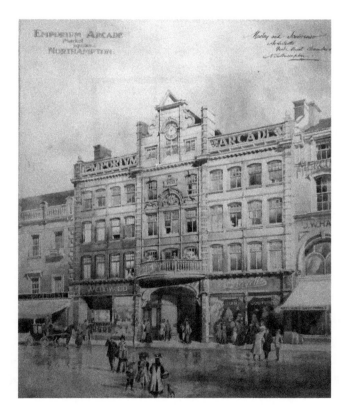

A watercolour by architects Mosley and Scrivener of the Emporium Arcade before it was built.

The prospectus included a sketch of the new frontage which closely represented what was eventually built, it suggests both that the development was to be named 'Central Arcade', and that W.T. Church might be one of the tenants. The watercolour, produced later by architects Mosley and Scrivener gave a beautiful representation of the Market square frontage with entirely fictional names for shops. The name 'Wedgwood' over the right-hand shop led to a later misunderstanding that this was an actual representation of the shop front after the occupation of Church's China.

In August 1901 an article in the Northampton Mercury gave a detailed description of the building as it neared completion. *'The materials used in the front are red local bricks with Weldon stone dressings, and an open work parapet of York stone acting as a permanent sign showing the words 'Emporium Arcade'. The central entrance is of Doulton's Carrara faience in white green and purple to special design and gives a note of colour to the lower part of the front. ...'*

Plans for a covered market had gone, but that would be built some years later at the junction of Sheep St and Bradshaw St. The opening of the Emporium Arcade before Christmas 1901 would doubtless have attracted a huge amount of local interest. It was Northampton's first covered, purpose-built shopping centre. Initially, it was well occupied, including at least one china shop, Tye & Sons, but W.T. Church stayed put in Sheep St.

William Wesley Church

William and his younger brother Wilfrid had much in common. They inherited the values of their parents: non-conformist in religion, abstaining from alcohol, progressive in politics and with a love of chess and walking. They both, at different times, wrote diaries, without which this book would have been much more difficult to write.

William took his principles and pursuits much further than did his brother. His walks were longer and faster, his pacifist and vegetarian principles were more strict, and he played chess harder and better. His diaries were full of fine details of chess and draughts matches, with the precise times and distances of long-distance walks, of interest probably to no-one but himself.

An eye lost in a childhood accident gave William, according to his brother, *'an unsteady glance and an expression of a shy approach'.* Wilfrid went on to describe him as an introvert, but *'steadfast to a fault'.* He worked as a clerk for Northampton Borough Council, becoming the chief clerk in the health department. He joined his father as a member of Northamptonshire Chess Club, taking up several offices in the club. He played draughts too. He also shared his parents' love of music, playing the piano and the church organ. He never married, living with his parents at 27 Holly Rd and later with his unmarried sister Dora at 15 Church Way, Weston Favell.

YMCA Draughts Club, winners of Northampton Town League 1909-10
William seated to the right of the Draughts board.

William took his vegetarianism beyond just not eating meat. He wouldn't wear leather-soled shoes and only ate eggs which he knew had not been fertilised. The word 'vegan' was not used until the 1940's, after he had died, but it is how his family remembered him. He belonged to a Vegetarian Association in Northampton and in January 1909 he arranged a concert for the association in which he played the piano.

William's long-distance walking was extraordinary. Sometimes it was for speed, sometimes for distance. *'Almost any day, winter or summer'*, wrote Wilfrid *'he would leave the Health Office where he was chief clerk, to take devious strolls into the countryside. His was a steady heel-and-toe stride of four miles an hour speed. … Seemingly time and distance were his main objects but surely he must on many occasions have been impressed by the peace and attractiveness of his surroundings.'*

An example of his speed was demonstrated by a twenty mile walk organised by Northampton & County Amateur Athletic Club on 21st July 1904 from Bedford to Northampton. William was one of 13 entrants. The Northampton Mercury reported that it was a very hot day, none of the competitors showed any sign of distress, but only seven finished the race, all in under 4 hours. *'A great crowd assembled on the Market Square to witness the finish, and all the walkers were heartily cheered.'* William finished second in a time of 3 hours 25 minutes and 50 seconds, four minutes behind the winner.

An example of long-distance walking was a fortnight's holiday recorded in his diary in 1914. He left Northampton at 4.10pm one afternoon and walked to Banbury, having forwarded his luggage by train to Chepstow. The following morning, he took the train from Banbury to Gloucester, from where he walked over successive days via Chepstow, Rhayader, Aberystwyth and Borth to Barmouth. He stayed there for a few days during which time he climbed Snowdon, and then walked home, stopping overnight in Dolgellau, Welshpool, Shrewsbury, Lichfield and Tamworth, 467 miles in 15 days.

He was interested in progressive social ideas but was never active in party politics. His pursuits demonstrated a lively and inquiring mind. Just before the outbreak of war he refers in his diary to attending a meeting of The League of Progressive Thought at the Divan Café to hear a lecture on Jean Jacques Rousseau, and then a little later at the same venue a talk on 'Human Developments in Relation to Language'.

Wilfrid Spencer Church

While William Church's pastimes can be traced by articles in the local press about chess and walking, his brother Wilfrid seemed to be less exceptional. He enjoyed walking, but not at the same speed or for the same distances as his brother. He travelled widely, taking adventurous touring holidays in Britain, and after the war, overseas.

He carried on the family tradition of abstinence from alcohol, was a vegetarian without the veganism of his brother and joined his father at College St Baptist Church before later moving to the Congregational Church in Abington Avenue. He was active in the Church Sunday School and a Captain of the Boys' Brigade. As a member of the YMCA, he took part in a cycle ride in 1906 to Cardiff. The following year he practised his debating skills in a mock parliament. He was a member of Conservative 'government' as President of the Board of Trade, while the future Labour councillor W.J. Bassett-Lowke was a Conservative President of the Local Government Board.

Like the rest of the family, he showed an interest in progressive politics and current affairs, more as an observer than a participant, but throughout his life he always sought, quietly and without fuss, to live by the principles he held.

Wilfrid tells us that he went to Spencer House School, Leicester Parade on the Barrack Rd. His earliest memory was being on a Sunday School procession to a celebration of Queen Victoria's golden jubilee on Northampton Racecourse. He was apprenticed at May's drug store in Welsh House. *'Business was bad, very bad'* wrote Wilfrid *'so Messrs. May drug store decided to move to a position somewhere south of London. An offer was made for me to accompany them but was not accepted. And so, I was glad to leave this occupation which had tied me to about ten hours a day with drudgery...'*

Wilfrid joined his father in the business in Sheep St. *'I drifted into this calling without much enthusiasm except for the 5s. at the end of each week which would be mine. The introduction to such a business as this is not very thrilling to a lad who has dreams of romance and adventure.'* He recalled that the business dealt consistently in all things ceramic and glass to such an extent that the stock included glass lamp shades, propagating glasses, red flowerpots and a cucumber glass for the propagation of straight cucumbers.

> *'How well I remember stringing a set of three jugs together and hooking them at the doorway priced at one shilling a set. It was a day out, too, to unpack a truck of pans and bread jars at the railway station siding.'*

A new shop assistant

In the early 20th century shopworkers never enjoyed any great status, being mostly single women working long hours on low pay. Many were treated like domestic staff, required to live above the shop, abide by strict rules and share cramped quarters with other staff and the proprietor's family. Wilfrid Church wrote; *'...there were shop assistants earning incomes of only twenty-five pounds a year on the 'living in' system.'* Not only was the renumeration atrocious but the hours of labour would be 8am to 6pm. In pointing out that *'these conditions existed in The Drapery of our own town'* he probably had one particular shop assistant in mind.

Naomi Johnson came to Northampton to work for Brice's, a clothes shop in The Drapery, also W.T. Church's landlord in Sheep Street. She was born in Isleham, a village in the Cambridgeshire Fens. Like most shopworkers, she did not come from a well-to-do background. Her father was a painter and her mother died when she was only nine years old, but with seven older sisters, there was a large and close family to take care of her. By the time she arrived in Northampton, Naomi was already experienced in shop work and used to living on the premises. She had worked in her brother-in-law's grocery shop, close to her home village. She left home to work in a clothing shop in Stamford, where, as was the custom, she lived above the shop, sharing, not just a room with her fellow employees, but sometimes a bed too. Naomi related how she was sacked by her employer for laughing in the shop. Her next stop was Furley & Hassan's, a well-established business in Oakham, before she arrived at Brice and Sons, Northampton.

Naomi recalled that before she knew Wilfrid, she used to admire a handsome young man who walked past Brice's every day taking Church's shop takings to the bank. She made a good impression on him and they became friends.

A more serious relationship started in 1908. Wilfrid wrote to Naomi several times while he was taking the Boys Brigade on holiday in Scarborough. She was then still living in Friendly House, 43 The Drapery, the home of Brice and Sons, while Wilfrid was living with his parents in Holly Rd.

Things were not going well in the business. Year on year sales from 7 Sheep St. drifted slowly downwards from £1,315 in 1906 to £1,248 in 1909. The cost of purchases meanwhile was increasing, up from £648 to £763, a trend that obviously couldn't continue. Wesley was losing interest, spending more time playing chess on his allotment. If the business was to survive, it needed to change, and Wilfrid needed to provide a secure home for any future wife and family.

Back to The Parade

Number 11 The Parade was a new shop fronting the Market Square on the right-hand side of the Emporium Arcade. The first occupant was Whiting & Co., who sold pianos and organs, competing directly with the long-established Abel & Sons who traded a couple of doors away. Perhaps that was the reason they moved to Abington St. in 1907. Wilfrid said that his father showed little interest when he suggested that they take it on. Wesley was losing any interest in the business, and without Wilfrid it would probably have closed at this time. However, Wesley didn't stop his son approaching the landlords. So, on September 17th, 1910, a new shop was opened and the business, now known as 'Church and Son' was back to the site of Parade House.

The shop in Sheep St continued, and the monthly takings for both were separately recorded. During 1910, the takings had averaged about £55 per month. The Parade shop took £83 in October, its first full month trading, while Sheep St. dropped to £41. The following year the whole business turnover was consistently over £100 per month, mostly from sales at the Parade. The obvious decision was taken to close the Sheep St. shop in June 1911 with an auction. Wilfrid wrote *'These three days actually represented a giveaway sale as only £100 6s 3d was realised, a very disappointing amount.'* In that first full year of trading from The Parade, the total sales of the business were £2,269 compared to just £1,248 in 1909.

Wilfrid and Naomi were now able to plan a wedding and a new family home. Naomi began working at Church's and moved into her future in-laws' home at 27 Holly Rd. In the summer of 1910 Wilfrid took a group of the boys brigade on a camping holiday at Hunstanton in Norfolk, writing regularly to Naomi about the difficulties of managing a group of unruly boys on holiday.

Just as they were planning the disposal of 7 Sheep St, Naomi heard that her elderly father was seriously ill. She returned to Isleham on May 21st, just in time for her to be with him when he died on May 24th. David Johnson's age of seventy was pretty good for a rural labourer at that time, but there was one genetic trait that repeatedly shows up in Naomi's family – longevity. Her mother may have died young, but her maternal grandfather died at 89, her great grandfather and an uncle both lived to be ninety. This was a family of poor rural labourers, not expected to live long lives. The genes carried on into Naomi's generation and beyond. Naomi's had eight sisters and two brothers. One of her brothers was seriously disabled due to a childhood accident and died young, the other emigrated to Canada in his youth to work on the Great Western Railway and returned to the UK for the first time, aged nearly 90, in the 1960's. He died aged 96. Of her sisters, all but two lived to be over ninety. Living to the age of 103, Naomi was to be the longest lived of them all.

Wilfrid and Naomi planned their wedding for September in Cambridgeshire, but some of Naomi's sisters urged that it should be postponed out of respect to their father. Naomi spent most of August preparing for the wedding with her sister Ada and her husband at their home in Exning, a few miles from Isleham. Wilfrid spent the month supervising the re-decoration of their new home in Ennerdale Rd, Spinney Hill. The house was then in open countryside, a couple of miles from the town centre. He wrote to her almost daily while they were apart. Some of Wilfrid's letters hint at his disapproval of Naomi's older sisters. It wasn't just the untimely date of the wedding so soon after their father's death that concerned them, Naomi was moving away from Cambridgeshire to marry a man whom they thought rather odd. He wrote to her: –

'I agree with your sisters (just fancy!) when they say that a small cake would be worse than none, and so it would be too; I am sure it will be better to forget all about the cake and look upon it as an unnecessary evil. The wedding is of course to be a quiet one, and no-one will be allowed to sing comic songs in the chapel, or to faint, it wouldn't be becoming.' Wilfrid then dropped the sarcasm and took a more direct approach 'You say that you and your sisters do not understand each other. Thank goodness you are not like them or you might see eye to eye with them,' then this frank admission 'Yes, you are an oddity, we both are, that's why being both odd (like one and one) we shall be even when married.'

On the wedding day, Wilfrid, his parents and sisters Hilda and Dora, travelled to Exning by train. True to form, William, or Billy as Wilfrid refers to him in the letters, preferred to walk. The Northampton

Mercury reported that the wedding at Exning Wesleyan Church was of a 'quiet character' due to the death of the bride's father. The story passed down by the family is that Naomi's sisters all wore black.

The newlywed couple left for a honeymoon at Penlee, a vegetarian guesthouse on the South Devon coast near Dartmouth and so began a lifelong attachment to this area. On their return, Wesley had completed the sale of the business to his son. Wilfrid wrote: *'By this time my father had ceased to take any active interest in affairs but assumed as it were a quiet and paternal watch over our progress. He represented a member of the past generation, meditative and anxious.'* The business name changed again to Church's China Stores and they had every reason to think that more prosperous and settled times lay ahead.

A circus visits town shortly after Church's move back to the Market Square.

CHAPTER FOUR

A FAMILY FOR PEACE

"I have never thought, for my part, that man's freedom consists
in his being able to do whatever he wills, but that he should not,
by any human power, be forced to do what is against his will."
Jean-Jacques Rousseau, Reveries of the Solitary Walker

ON 23RD FEBRUARY 1914, SIX MONTHS BEFORE THE OUTBREAK OF war, William Church attended a lecture on the 18th century French philosopher Jean-Jacques Rousseau. If the lecture included any reference to 'Reveries of the Solitary walker', the last and uncompleted work of the great philosopher, the title would have struck a chord with William, and by the end of the war, so would this quote.

The family had entered a settled period. Wesley, moving into his 60's, began a well-deserved retirement. He had more time for chess and the allotment, but Sarah began to develop arthritis, and from now on she would become increasingly disabled. The business move back to the Market Square under his son Wilfrid's management continued to be a success, with turnover continuing to grow from £2,020 in 1912, to £2,135 in 1913 and £2,315 in 1914. The newly-weds settled into suburban family life in Spinney Hill, and their first daughter, Joy, was born on August 20th, 1913.

Wesley's eldest son William continued his clerical work at the council, filling his spare time with walking, chess and music. In March 1914, he went to see a flying exhibition in Delapre Park. *'Three people were taken up'* he wrote *'and an exhibition of 'looping the loop' was given and during this for some time Mr Hucks flew upside down.'* On 27th June he walked to the home of Lord Henley at Watford Court (near Long Buckby) for a chess tournament. *'We had tea at Lord Henley's House and afterwards were photographed'.* Watford Court is long gone, but the photograph survives.

Chess match at Watford Court. William is standing on the far right, his father Wesley behind with a buttonhole flower.

The outbreak of war

On August 2nd William's diary contains a rare reference to international affairs. *'Serious news as to the outbreak of war between Germany and Russia. Austria, Serbia, Italy, France and possibly England all seem to be involved'*. The following day he took the train to Llandudno for a walking holiday, most of his fellow passengers were troops being mobilized around the country.

The news on August 7th that the Germans were reported to have lost 20,000 men at Liège, so early in the war, must have fed the belief that the war would be short. As usual, William doesn't record his feelings, just facts, and even those are annoyingly patchy.

These are some of the first few entries from what is left of William's diary. Edited by Wilfrid after his death, it is the only first-hand record, apart from a handful of official records and newspaper articles of the family's wartime experiences. It has a wider value as a personal record of conscientious objection in the First World War. William was not alone; both his brother and his father played their part in opposing compulsory national service too.

In September there was a sudden and dramatic arrival in the town.

An Army occupies Northampton

Northampton this week has been invaded. Thousands of soldiers from the western counties and from Wales have been drafted into Northampton to be trained for active service. Wherever one goes one sees troops. In nearly every street of the town soldiers are billeted, and the householders of Northampton have shown their patriotism by the cheerfulness with which they welcomed their enforced guests.

Every public hall, the schools of churches and chapels, the Technical School, all are occupied by troops, and the men stationed there have to sleep on the floor. Others are billeted in private houses, some of the streets in the town having soldiers in every house, and, generally speaking, these are the more fortunate ones, for they have a chance of a soft bed.

The coming of the troops

Exactly half an hour after noon on Sunday the 'occupation' of Northampton began. A long train crept quietly into the coal yard of Castle Station, and those who for two hours had struggled to retain balances on high walls were rewarded with a sight of the khaki they had waited for.

The news was conveyed in shrill tones by the adventurous boys to the crowd, numbering several hundred, which had assembled outside the Black Lion Hill entrance to the yard, and people craned their necks for a glimpse of the town's new guests. They were not kept waiting, for the doors swung back to admit a view of a long line of brown figures, which, to the accompaniment of a bugle band and clouds of dust, were advancing towards the street. …

Stiffened by training and bronzed through exposure, the troops marched briskly, despite their heavy personal equipment, to which were added the effects of a broiling sun. Nearly every man was smiling, and in many cases the weightier his luggage the broader the smile. …

Scenes in the town

Wherever one goes, in main and back streets, on the Racecourse or other open spaces, one sees soldiers, generally at work of some sort, in preparation for a time when their duties may have to be carried out in a hostile country, with the enemy's shrapnel bursting overhead.

Northampton Mercury Friday 4th September 1914

With the arrival of 17,000 troops, war fever had gripped the town. The same paper reported a call to arms by Earl Spencer and other members of the aristocracy to support Lord Kitchener's appeal for young men to sign up.

The Racecourse, just a few yards away from Holly Rd, had become the main army camp in town. The Church family welcomed two Red Cross territorials, billeted with them until the end of November.

Subsequent reports in the local press talk about special concerts put on for the visiting troops, of the Welsh language being heard in the streets and the warmth and hospitality with which the troops were received. The call to arms was thrust into the daily lives of the Church family as the press called upon every young man to do his duty for the country. The suffering of the war was also coming closer to home. William wrote of the bombing raid on Hartlepool, killing one hundred people. The losses of troops on the front were reported daily in the newspapers.

William noted that, as the Welsh troops left Northampton on December 21st, the town lights were dimmed to prevent the danger from Zeppelin bombs.

As the troops left, others were arriving, in smaller numbers and often in family groups that would stay for longer. They were refugees from Belgium. The families were housed by church members and special committees were formed for the purpose of taking care of them. The Mayor of Northampton launched a Belgian Relief fund with an appeal for donations. Wesley and William were listed in the Northampton Independent on 17th October 1914 as contributing ten shillings. On 3rd January 1916 William Church helped at a new year social event for the refugees in the town hall, hosted by the Mayor. He played a piano solo.

The Call to Arms

Millions of young men had taken up the call to arms. The pressure was particularly intense upon unmarried men; if they were seen in the street but not in uniform, they were a target for suspicion. A letter in the Chronicle and Echo in January 1915 headed 'Khaki Boys and Shirkers' called on 'shirkers' to be *'slighted'* to *'shame them, if possible, from propping up street corners or parading the streets.'* The letter drew a furious response in defence of people whose non-military work was essential to the war effort or who had been refused enlistment for health or family reasons.

The tone of hostility towards those who did not voluntarily enlist grew during 1915. In July, the commander of the Northamptonshire

Volunteer Training Corps wrote to local MPs objecting to new rules which required his corps members to enlist into the full-time army. *'We feel very strongly'*, he wrote *'that the unmarried shirkers and slackers outside the Volunteer movement should be subjected to recruiting pressure of this sort before married men of over 45, who are already drilling and willing to help in Home Defence in any part of the country.'*

In August a national registration scheme of all people of military age was launched. The Church family would have seen a report in the Chronicle and Echo on 30th September 1915 of a speech given by Kitchener to Labour leaders. *'It was not a question of raising an army of the required size'* he said, *'It is raised, and more than raised, already. The problem is to keep up a sufficient supply of trained men to fill up the gaps and make good the wastage from casualties.'* He went on to propose a ballot system of compulsory enlistment in every district that failed to supply the required quota of recruits. The paper carried a weekly record of people killed and injured on the front, people 'wasted' and in need of replacement.

The following day, a recruiting rally was held on the Market Square. *'Many thousands of people flocked to the square'* reported the Chronicle & Echo *'The five torchlight processions- starting from near the Racecourse on Kettering Rd, Far Cotton, Queens Park, Abington Park & St. James- all reached the Market Square within a few minutes of half past seven.'* Each procession was led by a band, and as they arrived in the Market Square the bands *'were massed in front of the Arcade, where they played patriotic airs until the meeting commenced.'* Earl Spencer presided over the meeting, and there was a succession of speeches by local political and military leaders. Sir Henry Randall declared it to be the greatest meeting in the history of Northampton.

The Chronicle and Echo reported that the speech by Charles McCurdy, one of Northampton's two MP's was particularly rousing. He *'reached a flight of lofty eloquence which he has seldom surpassed in Northampton.'* He told the crowd that *'last week the French and British Armies had begun to blast and pulverise their way through to Berlin.'* The newspaper's report of his speech concluded with the following.

'There has been a lot of discussion about voluntary service or conscription and all he would say about that is that Northampton should send forward the men. "I have always believed myself," he said "we can get them by the voluntary system, but I would never shirk from any method that becomes necessary to find the men. But here in Northampton, speaking as your senior member, I know I can make this offer to Lord Kitchener. Tell Northampton how many more men you want from the borough for the war, tell me what trades are not to be touched and how many men may be taken from the trades in which you wish recruiting to proceed, and I will answer for it that whenever the war office tell us plainly how many more recruits they want we will find the men from Northampton."

Honour and Glory

'He did not appeal to young men to join the army as a matter of duty. It was the glorious privilege that youth conferred upon them at the present time. They might as well be dead as be out of it. …

'The whole world was pulsating with the thrill of war, and those who by reason of age or other cause could not take part could not flatter themselves that they were in the stream of life coursing through the veins of Europe today. This was a great day for youth. The great adventure lay open before them. They came into the world with but one life to live and one end certain: that is death. They had the chance to lift their lives out of "the shallows and the miseries" to the heights of human endeavour, to breast the flood tide of fortune and to breathe the mountain air of freedom. He hated war and hoped this would be the last war he would see (hear, hear), but he recognised amid all the horror of it, there were pathways to honour and glory, sure and certain pathways to glorious life and, if it so pleased God, to a glorious death.'

In November the 'Derby Scheme' was introduced. It required every eligible man aged 18 to 41 who was not in an essential occupation to indicate his willingness to serve when called. Canvassers were sent to knock on doors and every man was required to attest to the canvasser whether he would join the forces. If he attested, he was then asked to go to the recruiting office within 48 hours. The process identified 318,553 medically fit single men across Britain, of those, 38% had refused to enlist.

There is little recorded in William Church's diaries in 1915. Doubtless the family watched appalled at the growing fever for war. They must have loathed Charles McCurdy's speech. Wesley, William and Wilfrid were people of strong principle, but they were not political leaders or activists. They were simply citizens who wished to live their lives according to their principles and contribute to the wellbeing of their community accordingly. Both brothers would have been canvassed and would have refused to enlist, but Wilfrid was married with a small child. The pressure was more on William. His last diary entry for the year was a report of a choir festival where he performed in *'three of four anthems and three solos, got on better than expected'*; nothing about pressure to enlist.

Conscription

Efforts to promote voluntary recruitment had failed to produce the troops needed. So, on 5th January 1916 Prime Minister Asquith put a bill before Parliament introducing conscription. On January 11th, William attended a meeting at the Northampton Friends Meeting House *'to consider what should be done by those who are standing out against the Government's compulsion bill. The men affected gave their reasons for resisting and suggestions were offered.'*

On January 22nd William's fast walking with friends caused a minor incident:

'Walked to Towcester and was stopped here by a police superintendent who enquired if we had gone through Towcester earlier in the

afternoon. We told him then he informed us we had created rather a sensation as we had been seen going across the fields near the station at a good pace and had been mistaken for escaped German prisoners. The roll had been called at the prisoners' camp, but none were missing. After some questioning, we were allowed to proceed.'

The Military Services Act became law on 27th January 1916. It stated that all unmarried men aged between 18 and 41 'be deemed as from the appointed date to have been duly enlisted in His Majesty's regular forces for general service…'. There were grounds for exemption, including work that was in the national interest or ill health. One reason for exemption, added to placate the widespread opposition to conscription, was conscientious objection to the undertaking of combatant service. Local tribunals were to be set up to determine applications for exemption. As the Northampton Chronicle and Echo correctly pointed out 'the men to whom the act applies… automatically become soldiers in the eye of the law.'

The national No Conscription Fellowship had been founded some months earlier. A group was formed in Northampton and William attended a meeting on March 5th. That night he was woken by the sound of a Zeppelin raid.

'Two warnings by the hooter at the electric works that enemy aircraft were about were given today… A good deal of stir was caused and at many of the churches and chapels services were abandoned in the evening. Some bombs were evidently dropped at a distance as on at least three occasions I felt a slight concussion and the windows of my bedroom shook.'

Subsequent reports were that the bombs dropped many miles away, near the coast and in the north-east.

The conscription tribunals were quickly constituted and put to work. Those who sought exemption were asked to submit their application forms to the Town Hall by March 2nd. Most of the cases heard were appeals for exemption on employment or medical grounds. It was not until the middle of March that the first applications on grounds of conscientious objection were heard in Northampton.

William attended another meeting of the No Conscription Fellowship on 19th March. He knew his case would be coming soon. On 22nd March he accompanied T.S. Smith to his tribunal to observe and take notes. Smith was recommended for non-combatant service, and he appealed.

William received notice of his tribunal on March 26th. He had three days to prepare, and on 28th he attended another meeting of the No Conscription Fellowship to discuss his tribunal the following day.

'March 29th, 1916. Attend the tribunal today to claim absolute exemption from military service owing to my conscientious objection to taking life and to taking part in warfare. My case was down for about 11am but actually came on about 3.10 pm. I heard other cases first and could see there was little hope of absolute exemption, as when the tribunal was satisfied there was a sincere conviction, they offered non-combatant service. I received the anticipated decision after a rather lively 5 minutes with questions.'

The local newspaper report did not name William as the applicant, but it gave a little more insight into his lively 5 minutes, showing his refreshingly argumentative streak.

'Would object to being killed

'A Clerk in a Corporation Department, who appealed as a conscientious objector, stated he has an instinctive dislike to militarism. He is a vegetarian.

"A rather unfortunate phrase isn't it?" Mr Geldart asked.
- "I don't think so", the applicant replied "Why?"
Mr Geldart: "Because the common or garden ground for that is cowardice."
- "No it is not, do you know what instinct means?"

Mr Geldart: "I believe it is animal sense."

- "Instinct is a feeling you cannot give reason for. It is in your nature."

Mr Geldart: "You have no objection to being killed have you?"

- "Yes of course I have."

Councillor Jackson: "Would you resist invasion?"

- "It depends what you mean by resist."

"Would you resist by force a landing of the Germans to take possession of this country?"

- "I should not take up arms against them, but I could not prevent them coming in. I should not attempt to kill them or to murder their wives or children, or that sort of thing."

The Chairman: "Would you attempt then to stop them murdering yours?"

- "So far as I could, peacefully. I should not take up arms to kill them."

"You would attempt to stop them by words."

- "Yes"

Mr Geldart: "Would you argue with them in German? Or English?"

- "I am an Englishman; I should argue in English. If they don't understand me I should get an interpreter."

'The appellant said that whether he was directed to combatant or non-combatant service the result would be the same: He would stick it out to the end. The Tribunal decided to give a certificate for non-combatant service.'

Unsurprisingly, William would keep his word to refuse non-combatant service, and he appealed against the decision. He was now one of a growing number of men around the country facing the consequences of their objection to military service, but they were not without support.

The national No Conscription Fellowship kept a record of every man using the conscience clause to seek exemption from military service. They were now a large campaigning organisation, with an office in London and a nationwide membership. On April 8th they organised a convention at Devonshire House, Bishopsgate, London. With public feeling was running high, there was a large police presence outside the hall. Delegates, including William Church and H.J. Turland representing Northampton, arrived through the back door, admitted by ticket only. The Globe, reflecting the opposition, said in its 'Notes of the Day' under the heading '*The Government and Open Sedition*': '*It is astonishing that such an organisation as the No Conscription Fellowship should be allowed to pursue its disloyal existence here in London. It is disgraceful that it should have the open assistance of certain members of Parliament. To-day it will hold a meeting. It is seditious. It should be proscribed.*'

There was a small demonstration outside the hall caused by a group trying to force their way in. A report in the Pall Mall Gazette said: '*They were persuaded to desist, but not before some of the stewards had thrown at them several bags of flour.*'

The press reported that 2,000 people attended the rally, William said about 500. The meeting was addressed by Philip Snowden, George Lansbury and Clifford Allen, who read a list of fifteen men who had already been handed over to the military authorities, with letters from some of them describing their resistance. '*Others of the letters written*' said the Pall Mall Gazette '*stated the determination of the writers never to perform any act of a military kind, no matter what the consequences. These letters were received with great cheering.*' A letter was read out from Ramsey MacDonald '*the way the conscientious objector had been treated was a scandal and a cynical commentary in all that was being said about liberty and freedom.*' Eventually, when loud cheering was heard outside the hall, the threat of disturbance led to the chairman asking that speakers were heard in silence. Mr Snowden got up to speak: "*Never since the days of Judge Jeffreys and the Bloody Assizes had there been such a travesty of justice as had been witnessed in the work of the tribunals." At this expression of opinion, the audience commenced to cheer*' reported the newspaper, '*but the chairman held up his hand "Hush!" as a reminder to his audience.*'

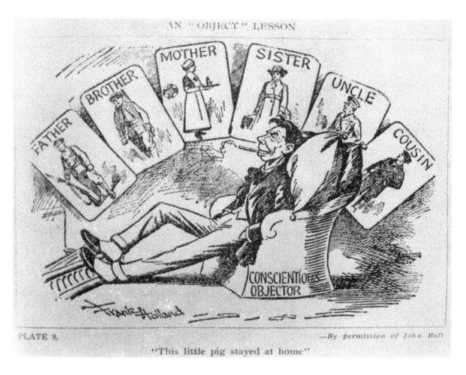

A First World War cartoon against 'shirkers'.

William reported the debate more than the speeches: *'Most of the discussion centred on alternative service in place of military service and there seemed to be a strong feeling against any compromise with the Government. ... The conference was resumed in the evening and resolutions against any compromise were passed by large majorities.'*

During the rest of April William was ill for some time. A note from Wilfrid in the diary says this was due to stress. On the 26th April he heard the happy news that he was an uncle again. Naomi had given birth to a second daughter, Irene.

On May 4th he attended a meeting of the Northampton No Conscription Fellowship in the Emporium Arcade to prepare for his appeal hearing the next day. The Northampton Mercury reported the hearing: -

A Corporation Clerk

William Wesley Church, chief clerk in the public health department of Northampton Corporation appealed against the decision of the Northampton tribunal, which had directed non-combatant service.

He said he had been in the Public Health Department for 18 years and had abstained from flesh food for sixteen years due to his objection to the taking of life. He thought he was doing better national service in his present position than he could do in any other way. He thought Belgium brought upon herself the treatment she received by offering resistance; she should have protested in the way Greece protested. If he was ordered into the Army he would go to prison, and, he supposed, remain there, until the end of the war.

Allowed 14 days to find definite work of national importance, such as the Friends' ambulance, etc. If appellant succeeds, he will be given a certificate, but if not the decision of the Northampton tribunal will be confirmed.

William's record of the appeal tribunal was that there was little difference to the earlier tribunal.

'...not much sympathy with the position of a conscientious objector was shown. I was given fourteen days in which to find work of national importance. Although my present job would certainly come under that head. The idea however seemed to be that I must make some sacrifice for my opinions.'

The future was now weighing heavily on William. He took a fortnight's holiday *'partly for the purpose of a rest and partly to seek out work of national importance. I may never attend the office again in my present capacity as an employee of the corporation. Resigned the secretaryship of the chess and draughts club at the YMCA.'*

On the 16th May, Wilfrid took his brother to Pershore to visit a fruit farm where he was offered a job for fifteen shilling a week, but William never took it up.

On 19th May, William was back in front of the tribunal. *'Attended the tribunal today and reported what I had been doing since the last meeting. They seemed very sympathetic this time and I was given another fortnight to find work of national importance.'* The Chronicle and Echo reported that William asked the chairman if the decision was unanimous. The chairman (Sir Stopford Sackville) replied *'I never heard such impertinence'*. *'I am not impertinent'* William replied. He reported in his diary, perhaps with a little glee, that he had managed to offend the chairman.

The next day, Harry Turland, who accompanied William to the No Conscription Fellowship rally in London, became the first conscientious objector in Northampton to be arrested.

In the next fortnight William attended several more No Conscription Fellowship meetings. He returned to work but had changed his mind on seeking alternative work of national importance. On June 2nd he appeared for the last time in front of the tribunal. *'I stated that I could not accept alternative service'*, he wrote *'and without allowing me to give reasons my appeal was dismissed.'* It's clear from the press report that William still wanted to make the case that his work at the Public Health Department at the Council was work of national importance. When he attempted to give his reasons the chairman said *'We do not want to know your reasons, we want to know what you have done'* The Clerk informed the committee that the *'appellant might easily have obtained work on the land in Northamptonshire if he had made any serious effort...'* His appeal was dismissed.

Arrest & Court Martial

William knew what was coming next. He knew that people before him had been arrested, handed over to the military, forced to wear uniform and court martialled for refusing to obey orders. The No Conscription

Fellowship were now producing a regular national publication 'The Tribunal', which set out what was happening to conscientious objectors after arrest. If William did not read The Tribunal, he probably heard about its contents. *'On May 7th a number of conscientious objectors who had declined to carry out military orders were taken to France'*, it reported on May 18th *'Having been transferred to France, these men have now automatically become liable to the death penalty for any disobedience to orders. We believe though that these men will be recalled this week.'* In fact, they were not recalled. A huge campaign against the threat of the death penalty was launched, but it was not until June 29th, well after William's arrest, that the full story of death sentences issued and then commuted to penal servitude became known.

On June 4th he wrote *'Last visit as organist at Commercial St. Chapel in case of call up by the military authorities.'* The next day: *'Received a notice from the barracks to present myself tomorrow, Tuesday to join the colours.'* He replied pointing out that he had attempted to explain to tribunals why he couldn't undertake military service, politely concluding *'I therefore have no alternative but to decline (with all respect to you personally) to comply with the matter.'*

In the evening he attended a meeting of the No Conscription Fellowship and the next day went to work as usual.

The following two days of entries in the dairy were short-hand notes written up some time later. They are reproduced here in their entirety.

'June 9th, 1916
'Sergeant Page arrested me this morning as an absentee under the Military Services Act but he waited until I had had breakfast before escorting me to the Police Station. I was treated very considerately. Had about an hour in the cell and was brought before the court at 10.30. I argued that my arrest was illegal owing to my not having received written notice of decision of County Tribunal until this morning. The argument did not avail, and I am to be fined £3 to be deducted from Army pay and was handed over to military escort.'

The hearing was reported in the Chronicle and Echo, and William once again made the point that no attempt had been made to inquire if his work at the council could be defined as being of national importance. When told that he was to be fined £3 he asked, *'Where is the £3 to come from?'* The Mayor: *'from your military pay.'* William replied that he would never accept any military pay.

The diary continued:

> *'Was taken to the barracks and refused to sign any papers and refused to undergo medical examination.'*

These papers survive today. In the space for the signature of the recruit is written in pencil 'refused to sign'. They show that he had been given exemption from combat service on conscientious grounds and under medical classification as to fitness for service is written 'refused examination'.

> *'My treatment here was very considerate but was only kept about two hours and was then sent off in charge of another escort by the 1.30 train to Seaford.'*

Seaford is on the Sussex coast, near Brighton, from where several CO's had been taken to France.

> *'A corporal was sent to carry the kit which had been allotted to me. He proved an excellent fellow and carried the kit the whole way, except that I assisted him with the overcoat when we reached Euston. I had in the escort all the advantage of a valet, without the expense. From Euston we went by tube to Victoria and I was asked once or twice for my ticket. It was a pleasant journey down and we arrived at Seaford at 6.30. There was a walk of about two miles to the camp and on arrival here there was a change of treatment.*
>
> *'My escort handed over a letter from the authorities and left me in their charge. On being instructed to take the kit over to the*

hut where I had been located I said that the kit did not belong to me, and there was an argument about the 'beastly Germans' and a threat that I should be sent over to France without anyone being acquainted with the fact. Finally, the kit was fastened round my neck and I was sent over to the hut.

'I found at this hut seven or eight very gentlemanly fellows who seemed however to be too plausible and affected. There were two others who seemed to be of the same mind as myself and I promised to post two letters for them at the GPO at Seaford. I then went to the town and posted the letters and also sent a postcard home. I then returned to the hut and had to sleep on a board without any mattress. I had a fairly good night however.

10th June 1916
'In the morning I am asked to put on khaki and did put the trousers on but refused to don the tunic. Some of the N.C.C.'s were ordered to dress me and this they did in a very nervous way. I was then taken to the barbers and my beard was shaved off. Two other fellows were brought in and forcibly dressed. At 10 am we were brought before the C.O. who warned us of the seriousness of disobeying orders and promised us light non-military work under pleasant conditions if we would acknowledge authority.

'Went with two other fellows (N. Thirtle and L.J. Holden) for a stroll near the top of the cliffs. When we returned, we found the two men who had been forcibly dressed (A.W. Walker and V.M. Pyle) arrested for disobeying orders and were in detention, and just after my two companions suffered a similar fate leaving me the last of the five.

'I had just had dinner when I was ordered by a sergeant to scrub a table. I refused, and directly after another sergeant gave me similar orders and warned me of the consequences of refusal. I again refused and was taken to the detention room and my pockets were emptied. I was cordially received by the other four.

*The guard room was quite bare of any furniture and contained
four windows. It was about twenty-three feet square. We passed
the time as pleasantly as could be expected and had arguments
and games until bedtime. We had to sleep on the floor without
mattresses or pillow and had only two blankets.'*

One thing would give William some comfort. Unlike some of his
fellow conscientious objectors, he knew that he had the support of
his family, and that they would be taking up his cause. On the day
after his son's arrest Wesley Church wrote to W. Long MP, President
of the Local Government Board, and he copied the letter to the
Northampton Daily Echo.

Dear Sir,

*I feel I can write to you with confidence, knowing from experience
the personal character of your esteemed family for justice and
equality (I was resident at Devizes for more than ten years,
which town you now represent in Parliament).*

*Yesterday I had the painful experience of visiting my son in
a prison cell at the police station, placed there by the military
authorities, illegally, I think.*

The facts of the case are these: -

*He was in an important post of trust- chief clerk to the
County Borough of Northampton in its Health Department, and
during the visit of the 20,000 troops to the town he fulfilled those
duties with success. This post he held for 18 years, until he was
arrested yesterday.*

*He appealed first to the Borough and then to the County
Tribunal for exemption from military service on conscientious
grounds.*

*They both recognised his sincerity and gave him exemption
conditionally. The conditions of the first Tribunal were that he
take non-combatant service. He objected to military service of
any kind.*

The conditions of the second Tribunal were that he obtains some employment of national importance, but they also insisted (illegally, I think), that he should give up his present useful employment to take up some other employment of less importance. Of course, he resisted, and the consequences were- he was placed in a prison cell, handed over to the military, and yesterday was sent to Seaford by the 1.25pm train.

He will resist all orders of the military authorities, and you know the result. Is this action fair, reasonable or just?

Yours sincerely,

Wesley T. Church

Wesley had not done his research properly. Walter Long was not the MP for Devizes. He was the Conservative MP for Strand, in the heart of London. He came from a wealthy landowning family in Wiltshire and had previously been the MP for North Wiltshire, but never for Devizes. As a traditional Conservative he was unlikely to be sympathetic to Wesley's plea, and the reply from the board was 'that they could not see the way clear' to advise him.

William's entries in his diaries were always understated. He rarely complained about his treatment, reporting his conditions in a straightforward, factual manner. For the next week, he was incarcerated in the guardroom at Seaford barracks, sharing a small space not just with other conscientious objectors but any soldiers in trouble with the authorities. At 11 o'clock one night two drunks were thrown in. Some of the prisoners received fruit and cake from home which they shared around. *'If it had not been for this'* said William *'I should have had to have lived principally on bread, margarine and tea.'* The next day seven more CO's arrived from Norwich, so 20 were sleeping in the guardroom floor that night.

On June 16th nine were taken for medical examination, and some had to be forcibly stripped. One of them was *'roughly handled'* wrote William, *'three of the four buttons were torn off his tunic.'* On June 18th they were marched out and told that they would be court martialled the next day. They were allowed to prepare a statement in writing.

> *June 19th- 'Court martial came off this morning. Was not allowed to put in testimonials as to character and had to simply admit that I had disobeyed orders, so I had not much of a case. Handed in my written statement however.'*

The next day William was transferred to a different guardroom; the conditions were, he says, much better. *'Guards decent fellows and food more plentiful.'*

On June 21st the result of the court martial was announced. The sentence for nine of them, including William, was 112 days imprisonment with hard labour.

They left by train for Maidstone prison 7.40 the next morning with five guards. They reached their destination at 3pm, by which time *'our escort was now on the border of intoxication'* said William. *'I am afraid the prisoners had been too generous'*. Another touch of William's sarcasm. As he arrived in prison, he was allowed to write home, his letter was reported in the Northampton Daily Echo under the heading 'Still Smiling'.

"STILL SMILING!"

Mr. W. W. Church Court-Martialed.

112 DAYS' HARD LABOUR.

Mr. W. W. Church; the chief clerk in the Northampton Corporation Health Department, who was arrested a fortnight ago as a conscientious objector, went from Northampton to Seaford, near Newhaven. There he disobeyed military orders and was under detention for ten days. He was tried by a court-martial and was sentenced to 112 days' imprisonment, with hard labour.

In a letter home, he says, " Still smiling!"

On the Chairman ordering the Court to be cleared for the consideration of a case at the County Appeals Tribunal, to-day, Mr. W. T. Church, father of W. W. Church, approached the table and said, " I wish to tell you the result of the sentences you have passed—"

The Chairman said Mr. Church was not in order in addressing the Tribunal, and they could not hear him.

We recently published a letter that Mr. W. T. Church sent to Mr. Walter Long, the President of the Local Government Board. He received a formal acknowledgment, with the intimation that the Board "could not see their way clear" to advise him in the matter.

Mr. Church tells us that he is writing to-night to Mr. McCurdy, Mr. Lees Smith, and Mr. Philip Snowden.

Northampton Daily Echo
23rd June 1916.

'On arrival at prison a few particulars as to religion were taken, and we were examined by the doctor and placed in a small cell where we received our supper of one pint of porridge and eight ounces of brown bread. At about 7pm we were transferred to our cells and I was placed in C3-2.'

William's time in Maidstone prison from June 22nd to August 8th is recorded in one single diary entry. Once again, William's record is understated. He was in solitary confinement in spartan conditions with no allowance for his vegetarianism.

'In prison during this period and went through the usual routine. For the first week I slept without a mattress and after four weeks was allowed a library book, such as a novel besides the book termed of an educational order. A bible, a prayer book and a book called the Narrow Way were allowed from the time of admission.

'I had a good cell in the new part of the prison and found it easy to keep clean. The polishing of the tins etc. was more troublesome. I was put on coal sacks for the first few weeks and then transferred to mail bags, and after four weeks I was allowed to work in association with others.

'The warders with one or two exceptions were very decent fellows. From my cell window I had a good view of the surrounding country and of a small street (Camden Road, I believe), and I spent some time looking out of the window.

'The restrictions as to not talking and the ignorance as to any outside affairs was rather trying.

'As regards the meals there were three. Breakfast about 7.30am consisted of eight ounces of nice brown bread and one pint of gruel and supper at 4.20pm substituted porridge for gruel and these two meals were of course appetising to me. After the first few days dinner was more difficult and on four days out of seven, I had to be content with six ounces of bread and eight ounces of potatoes. On one day (Monday) I had ten ounces of haricot beans (which I had to wash out of bacon fat) in addition and on two days (Sundays and Fridays) I had a pint of soup but during the latter part of my treatment I refused the soup as I found meat scraps in it.

'I spent the time when it began to weigh heavily by

arranging in imagination walks to various country places around Northampton and once I had a weekend to Banbury. I also counted the number of weeks to my discharge day which was put down for Sep. 21st and also estimated the time when I should be able to write home and to receive an extra library book.

'Notwithstanding the restrictions on conversation we were able to exchange a few words when on exercise etc and all sorts of rumours as to the Home Office scheme for C.O.'s were afloat. On my arrival there were about thirty other C.O.'s and this number increased to about ninety. I soon picked out Turland and Craddock but after a few days Craddock was removed to hospital where he remained for the rest of the time. I was able to speak to Turland once or twice when on exercise. After about four weeks Sid Smith was admitted and I had a few words with him also and was once cautioned for this.

'We occasionally saw some of the convicts, some of whom were in for life and there were some rather repulsive faces among them. I did not attend chapel at all and received only two visits from the chaplain, one on admission and the other about a week before the discharge.'

Sidney Smith, referred to in this diary extract, had been in front of the Northampton Tribunal on June 30th. Sid might have had an opportunity to whisper when they met in Maidstone prison that William's father had interrupted his tribunal in his support. The Northampton Mercury reported: *'Mr W.T. Church rose from the body of the court, asking to be permitted to speak on the prisoner's behalf. He was immediately informed he had no right to make a speech and must sit down.*

Prisoner- Have I the right to call Mr. Church as a witness to my character? The magistrates clerk replied that he had not.'

This wasn't the first time Wesley had attended a tribunal after his son's arrest. He interrupted another tribunal seeking to tell them the result of the sentence on his son. He was refused permission to speak. He wrote to the local MP and to Mr Lees Smith and Philip Snowden. On Friday 21st July, Wesley travelled to Westminster with Harold Croft, a leading member of the Northampton No Conscription Fellowship and Mr J Pagesmith to lobby local MPs, Charles McCurdy and Harry Manfield on behalf of five imprisoned conscientious objectors from Northampton. They met, according to the Northampton Mercury, for an hour and a quarter.

Dyce Camp

In the first week of August, rumours circulated around Maidstone prison that a new scheme was being put together for conscientious objectors in prison. On August 8th William and about fifty others were moved to Wormwood Scrubs prison, which processed all the English prisoners considered suitable for the Home Office Scheme. They were told that if they accepted work of national importance they would be released from prison and placed under civilian control.

On August 10th they were returned to Maidstone and given papers to sign accepting a work scheme. On August 22nd William was one of 20 conscientious objectors released from prison *'We were dressed in typical navvies clothes'* wrote William *'and given, I believe 3s.8d. for our food for the day and were then told we were to proceed to Dyce near Aberdeen and to report to a Mr Curtis Gray.'* After the short train journey to London the group were left to themselves for a few hours before boarding the train to Scotland. *'We did not patronise high class establishments as our clothes seemed scarcely suitable to luxurious surroundings.'*

The train left Kings Cross at 11.45pm and the next morning they were in Scotland. *'...interested in passing over the Forth and Tay bridges and viewing the cities of Edinburgh and Dundee'* recalls

William. They arrived at Aberdeen and then took the short journey to the nearby village of Dyce, and a further two miles to some quarries. As usual, William sees the positive- *'Some pleasant woods and nice scenery including a view of the Grampians were close at hand and an ancient Druid circle (stone) was about half a mile away. The weather was very fine on arrival and conditions looked promising. About twenty tents were erected and we found accommodation to suit us, and after dinner in a marquee we were given three blankets each and a mattress and pillow which we had to fill with straw from a barn close by.'*

William's party were the second group to arrive at Dyce. More groups of a similar size arrived until there were about 250 men. They were to break up granite for road stone, take it in wheelbarrows to steam crushers and load the crushed chippings into trucks. They were paid 8d a day (about £2 at today's prices). *'We were at first expected to work on the quarry for five hours 2 shifts. The first shift were on at 7.00 until 9.30 and again at 1 until 3.30 and the second shift at 9.30 until 12 and 3.30 until 5.40. On Saturday worked stopped at 4 p.m. and every fourth Saturday at 12.'*

The views of the mountains soon disappeared as the weather changed. *'When rain set in as it sometimes did for a day or two at a stretch, we had an unpleasant time of it,'* wrote William. *'The sleeping tents were by no means watertight and a large proportion of the men removed to the village, to cottages, barns, etc.'* Those that did this had to do so at their own expense.

A young man called Walter Roberts was taken ill at the camp. The local doctor diagnosed a 'chill', but the following night Roberts fell from his bed and ended up lying on wet ground for two hours. The next day the doctor said he was too ill to be moved, no nursing was provided, and he died of pneumonia. His death led to calls for a public inquiry, and the camp was inspected. On the same day Ramsey MacDonald, Labour MP and future Prime Minister visited the camp. *'On Sept. 19th the Home Office Committee came down and made arrangements for us all to be removed to barns'* wrote William.

Out of prison, William was able to return to some of his old pursuits and keep his mind busy. He climbed a nearby mountain, Brynmoor, visited local villages and landmarks and regularly walked into Aberdeen to visit the theatre or cinema. He had tea at the Independent Labour Party rooms and attended some of their talks. He wrote that he was successful in chess and draughts tournaments at the camp.

On 14th October William wrote that a group photograph was taken. The photo still survives, but William remains elusive among the weatherworn and hollow cheeked faces.

That night '*a gale brought down both the recreation and the dining tents, we had to have makeshift meals in the barns until Monday afternoon tea-time.*' Maybe the authorities realised that conditions in a Scottish winter would be intolerable, and the risk of more deaths politically unacceptable, so on 24th October a notice was put up that work would cease the next day and they were to return home for eight days leave.

Conscientious objectors at Dyce Camp near Aberdeen.

On Leave

After an overnight stay in Aberdeen, William took the train back to Northampton, recording the changes and times with his usual meticulous detail. Arriving at Northampton station he was greeted by a small reception committee, including his father and members of the No Conscription Fellowship.

The next fortnight was spent visiting friends and the families of other conscientious objectors in Northampton. There was time for some walking, a visit to the council offices to meet former colleagues, a meeting of the Independent Labour Party in the Emporium Arcade and a small party at Wilfrid's house in Spinney Hill. *'A pleasant evening was spent, with recitations, songs, etc., A collection of 6d. each was made to go for a fund providing coal in a deserving case.'*

With the attention he had received in the local press, William was probably quite well known by now. If any hurtful remarks were made, he doesn't mention them. He does refer to one encounter, on a walk to Wellingborough: *'...met several factory hands and it seemed to astonish them to find me at liberty again. One man stopped and turned, saying "What – have you dodged 'em?"'*

Warwick prison

On 17th November William arrived at Warwick prison, which had been converted to a work camp for conscientious objectors. He was put to work on mailbags. William leaves no record of his living conditions at Warwick, but he and his comrades were free to travel widely. He attended lectures and public meetings in Leamington and Warwick, and the conscientious objectors met to discuss action in solidarity with conscientious objectors elsewhere suffering more difficult conditions. In Coventry William attended a meeting addressed by Phillip Snowden: *'All the C.O.'s were present in the gallery and Mr. Snowden expressed his pleasure at their presence and congratulated them on their attitude. The desire for an early peace was strongly expressed.'*

On December 5th William walked home from Warwick to Northampton, 34 miles in eight hours. He returned 5 days later, leaving Northampton at 11pm, walking overnight and arriving in Warwick at 7 o'clock in the morning. The next day, unsurprisingly *on one or two occasions felt rather sleepy.*

After another fortnight at Warwick, which included a lecture on J.S. Mill's 'On Liberty', William was granted leave over Christmas until New Year's Day. He spent Christmas week quietly, at home most of the while, and returned to Warwick on 1st January.

Dartmoor

The first two months of 2017 were spent at Warwick before William heard plans of another move. On 21st February it was announced in Parliament that Dartmoor prison was to be converted into a work camp for conscientious objectors, employed to reclaim land on the moors for agriculture. After a weekend break in Northampton, he heard that he was to be transferred there. Four days later, with his father and his sister Dora making the journey to Warwick to wish him well, he and seventy others set off by train. *'We had rather a warm reception at stations between Plymouth and Princetown,'* wrote William *'mostly from children however. We reached Princetown and had a very favourable impression of the place. I obtained a position in a cell only recently vacated by the convicts, and I found it clean, dry and comfortable.'*

William's group was one of the first to arrive at Dartmoor. As the settlement grew to over 1,000 men, so local opposition grew. On 22nd April a group of CO's visiting Tavistock were surrounded, and one was struck by a wounded soldier. Police were needed to restore order. One un-named but 'well-known' Tavistock resident told a reporter of The Western Times about his encounter with conscientious objectors on an earlier visit to Princetown *'I met a number of them'* he said *'going for a walk in the direction of Two Bridges. They were well dressed, had kid gloves and carried walking sticks in quite a "toffy" style.'* William

Church recorded a walk to Two Bridges on March 17th, but it is hard to imagine him meeting this description.

On 25th April a huge rally was held in Plymouth chaired by the Mayor to object to the conscientious objectors being housed in Dartmoor prison. Letters from local MPs were read out to cheers from the crowd. Typical of these letters was one from Sir C. Kinlock-Cooke MP who wrote *'Men imbued with views and ideas so pernicious in themselves, and so utterly opposed to the grand traditions upon which the British empire has been built up, are in my opinion beneath contempt.'*

Prominent local people spoke at the meeting to denounce the 'conchies'. Brigadier General F.G. Stone added some vicious words about CO's and Germans. *'We had said goodbye to the convicts who kept the prison clean, and they had been replaced by vermin who had made the prison too foul for a decent convict to enter it again. (Applause) He would a thousand times rather shake hands with most of the convicts than soil his fingers by touching one of these conscientious objectors (Hear, hear). They were the allies of Germany, – allies of the most brutal and degenerate nation on the face of the earth- a nation which in the 30 years war gave itself over to cannibals, and which, if the accounts were true, had now again resorted, though in a more scientific manner, to the same horrible vice.'*

The meeting passed a resolution *'That this meeting of Plymouth and the neighbouring district, summoned and presided over by his Worship the Mayor, hereby expresses its strong resentment at the liberties and privileges allowed to a large number of law breakers at Princetown, who have refused to perform their duty to their King and country, and are now permitted to shirk work and annoy the law abiding inhabitants of the district; and is of the opinion that unless these persons are confined within the grounds and precincts of the prison and the existing scandal of their lenient treatment ended, the natural indignation of his majesty's loyal subjects will undoubtedly lead to serious consequences.'*

After the invited speakers the Mayor called for contributions from the floor. A local non-conformist minister, Rev. W. Riley stood up to speak proposing an amendment to the resolution. *'Liberty loving and justice loving citizens of Plymouth'* he began, *'As a son of a Waterloo veteran who took many medals and served 15 years in the army, as the nephew of an uncle who died in the Crimean war, and the cousin of another who laid down his life for England in the Boer war and as the father of an only son who six months ago took the military medal in France, I wish to speak in favour of the men.'*

There was a few moments of stunned silence. *'...possibly a distrustful silence- gave place to the greatest disorder'* reported the Western Morning News *'Hissing and shouting rendered it impossible for Mr Riley to proceed'*. Despite pleadings from the Mayor the crowd refused to hear him. *'As the meeting broke up there was an ugly rush to get hold of Mr Riley as he left the hall. The police, who were in good force, came to his protection.'*

A few days later William heard Mr Riley and his daughter speak to a group of conscientious objectors at Dartmoor, but public pressure led to CO's being denied permission to enter any local towns except Princetown and rations were reduced.

Life at Dartmoor

William's diary of his time at Dartmoor consists mostly of references to long walks over the moors, together with occasional talks and concerts, often performed by his colleagues. He received letters and food parcels from his family and exchanged letters with other conscientious objector friends in prisons and work camps around the country. Most of the time the tedious routine may not have been worth recording. Other sources give a clearer picture of life there.

The conscientious objectors were paid eight pence a day, compared to a soldier's wage of one shilling. A major complaint seemed to be that the C.O.'s were free to spend this, and any money they had brought with them, in Princetown shops, depriving local people at a time when food was short.

Conscientious Objectors at Dartmoor Prison.

Work included quarrying and agriculture. Stone was quarried for a new road that became known as conchies road, or the road to nowhere. Others were put to work building a new boundary wall to a large tract of moor that was then ploughed and came to be known as 'conchies field.' Some dug drainage ditches which were reported to be far in excess of what was necessary. Others worked on the farm owned by the Duchy of Cornwall.

Lydia Smith of the Women's Committee of the No Conscription Fellowship visited Dartmoor and wrote this in a letter to the Manchester Guardian *'The agricultural work is penal in character, and it is organised on exactly the same lines as for convicts...The crushing of oats is performed with antiquated machinery of the treadmill type, except that hands are used instead of the feet. Sixteen men are required to use this machine and the output is six bags a day...I saw a gang of eight men harnessed to a handroller engaged in rolling a field...The barrows and spades are prodigiously heavy, with a view to tiring the* users, and all the appliances and methods are of the most antiquated nature. The coke in the gas works is transported by teams of ten men harnessed to a cart...The food is poor, and the hours of labour...are longer than those imposed on convicts.'

A fellow C.O. Walter Manthorpe recalled: 'was sent to dig in the garden and I did it and I went unconscious, that knocked me completely out. And then after that I was given a job of dealing with stones, stonework. And that was very difficult work to shape stones. You had to use a hammer and chisel to do that. And I was knocking on a piece of stone and one of the chips went completely into my wrist there and that was terribly painful, that was. And I had to have it taken out. And they'd got no anaesthetic or anything, they had to do the best they could with it. And I went out then, that sent me out, you see.'

William says very little about the work, for most of the time he worked indoors. On one occasion he said he was being transferred from the mattress department to the twining shed, on another that he was doing clerical work on the payment of wages, and on a third that he was put on haymaking, together with most of the other indoor workers, during August.

In early January 1918 he heard news that his brother was due to visit. Wilfrid was visiting a china and glass business that was for sale in Paignton on the south Devon coast. They arranged to meet on a bridge over the river Dart near Ashburton and walked to the summit of Ausewell Tor, where they enjoyed glorious views over the south Devon coast. William commented that it was the first time that he had seen any of his family since March 4th the previous year. 'Wilfrid looking well', wrote William 'he seems inclined to take on the business at Paignton', and so a new branch of Church's China began.

In February 1918 a sad event was to have major repercussions for the Dartmoor settlement. Henry Firth, a conscientious objector from Norwich died at Dartmoor of pneumonia. He had arrived on 31st December, having served nine months in prison elsewhere. He was described as a 'bag of bones', and without being examined by a doctor he was sent to work in the quarry. A fellow CO described him as 'broken in health both physically and mentally by long imprisonment, he was sent to work here on the bleak moors, at a time when the weather was at its worst and in spite of the fact that from the first he appeared to be in a dying condition. He was ordered to the Heavy Quarry Party; the change from confinement in a prison to the high bleak hills of Dartmoor was so sudden that the poor fellow suffered terribly from the cold and when too weak to work was charged with slacking. A number of times he endeavoured to get treatment at the hospital but was turned down with a sneer and a gibe about the 'men in the trenches'.'

The day after his death, the CO's met and passed the following resolution. 'This general meeting of members of the Dartmoor Settlement beg to inform the Home Secretary that they are ceasing work between 6am and 7pm on Friday, February 8th to mark their respect to their deceased comrade H.W. Firth, and their indignation at the treatment by the doctors in the Settlement Hospital. They further desire their cessation of work to be regarded as a protest against the general maltreatment of conscientious objectors in various prisons and settlement hospitals as a consequence of which a number of CO's have already had their ends hastened or their health permanently injured or undermined.'

On February 9th, William wrote: 'Walked in procession with about one thousand other C.O.'s to the station to accompany the remains of H. W. Firth to the train en route for Norwich. Ordinary members of the settlement preceded the coffin which was carried by C.O.'s, then came the Norwich men and finally members of the Committee. Just as the train left the station the hymn "Lead kindly light" was sung. Notice up at the gates stating that all men who ceased work on Friday were confined to settlement until further orders. Charge sheets were also sent to the majority of those remaining away from work.'

The confinement to the settlement was lifted on 22nd February, but the following day William reported that two of their number, C.H. Norman and H.P. Hughes, were handed over to the military authorities. C.H.Norman was sentenced to a year in prison with hard labour for organising the strike.

On 25th February William wrote:- '*Notice from manager that the result of charge against me was that I had been put into Class E for six weeks thus receiving 4d. per day instead of 8d for this period. The remaining 520 or so men were treated similarly.*'

On March 27th William received a letter from his father to say he was coming to visit. Wesley cycled from Tavistock, William set out to meet him and they walked back to Princetown, visiting stone circles on the way. Wesley lodged in Tavistock for three days, perhaps with Mr Wiggins who was visiting his son Leslie. One night the two fathers, their two sons and a third Northampton C.O., H. Craddock, all had dinner together in Princetown after visiting the cemetery of French and American prisoners of war held there over one hundred years earlier during the Napoleonic wars.

Despite claims in the press that conscientious objectors were getting free travel passes to return home on leave, William never once left Devon during his two years at Dartmoor. In the early period, the ban on visiting towns meant that he was only allowed to wander on the moor. In June 2018 he was accused of going 'out of bounds' and he was confined to the settlement for a month, but on that occasion, William doesn't record his route.

Life in Northampton

Back home, the Church family continued to live in an atmosphere of deep hostility to conscientious objectors. In August 1917, an unnamed man living in Mears Ashby sought exemption from military service on religious grounds. He was a 'colporteur' (a distributor of religious publications) and a lay evangelist for a Wesleyan chapel. Despite a letter of support from his minister, his application was refused.

A letter in the Northampton Mercury from a fellow Wesleyan, Mr Buffham, was critical of his conscientious objection. Wesley Church wrote a letter in response, supporting his application, and conscientious objectors in general.

Sir,- I am sorry Mr. Buffham has thought fit to throw stones at a conscientious objector, a colporteur from Mears Ashby, who appealed at the Wellingborough Tribunal last week, on conscientious grounds.

There are hundreds who are suffering imprisonment rather than submit to militarism in any form, and, I believe, are fully justified in the stand they have taken against the mad spirit of brutal war now being carried on by so many nations- so called Christian nations- of the earth.

It requires no argument of mine to prove that war is opposed to humanitarianism and civilisation. All are agreed on this point. But we have a higher motive than either if we profess Christianity and follow the teaching of our Saviour in his Sermon on the Mount.

If a better spirit had been manifested at the commencement of the war all the bloodshed and misery might have been avoided. The mistrust and fear then manifested would have been substituted for reasonable and just conciliation.

Victory gained by force will never bring lasting or satisfactory peace.

For these reasons and others many conscientious objectors are suffering intense persecution without complaint and are willing to suffer death than cause the death of another.

Yours,
Wesley T. Church
27, Holly Road, Northampton
August 25th 1917.

The local papers continued to report the daily toll of lives lost on the front, and the questions asked of young men still at home and not in uniform grew more intense. A designation of badged employment was used for those carrying out work essential to the war effort, including many Northampton people making boots for the army. A self-employed china and glass dealer such as Wilfrid Church would not get any such badge.

Family stories of the business being subject to boycotts, or white feathers being put through the letter box can't be verified. The takings of the shop showed steady growth throughout the war, rising from £2,314 in 1914 to £5,195 in 1918, but this was also a time of high inflation, 25% in 1917 and 22% in 1918. Things were going well enough for the shop to advertise for a 'strong lad' to assist in September 1916, but it seems that Wilfrid did not invest as much in advertising as he had done before the war.

In March 1916 a heavy snowstorm did some damage to the shop. A wire net over the glass lean-to roof at the back of the shop collapsed under the weight of snow, crashing through the roof. It was 4.30 in the afternoon and 'everything in the room was smothered' according to the Chronicle and Echo, but no-one was hurt.

Wilfrid had joined the St. Johns Ambulance and the Voluntary Aid Detachment soon after the start of the war. He had done work as a volunteer orderly at Northampton hospital, including transporting military and civilian wounded.

In October 1917 he applied for exemption from military service on the grounds both of conscientious objection and that 'hardship would ensue' for his wife, children and parents, his mother now being an invalid. He was granted temporary exemption until 22nd March 2018, which was then extended to 29th June. However, it was exemption from combatant service only, so he appealed to the County Tribunal and his case was heard in early June. He told the tribunal that he opposed military service because war is immoral and human life sacred, and because even non-combatant service assisted the military machine. He objected to the use of arms in any cause, however just.

Wilfrid pointed out that his voluntary work showed that he was prepared to be called out at any hour of the day or night, and he considered it to be work of national importance. He produced letters vouching for the sincerity of his views, but the local tribunal could not see why he could not carry out similar work in the army. The appeals tribunal, although it dismissed his case on grounds of hardship to his family, granted exemption on conscience grounds, on the condition he did three days a week in hospital Voluntary Aid Detachment work.

The war draws to a close

From the second half of 1918 there are very few entries in William's diary. On September 4th, he mentions Princetown's famous pony fair 'Sale of ponies at Princetown today and a large number of visitors came in. The C.O.'s were warned about exercising care in the evening, but as far as I know no disturbance occurred.' A couple of days later he records the vegetarians' superiority at chess: 'Played in a chess match Vegetarians v. Meat Eaters. Our side won by five games to one. '

In October, there was an outbreak of flu at the camp, a foretaste of the havoc it was to cause a few months later as the soldiers returned home. On October 25th he wrote 'A C.O. died from influenza in the hospital this evening. About thirty cases now under treatment.'

On November 11th he wrote:- 'Report arrived that an armistice with Germany had been signed and hostilities had ceased at 11 a.m. Germany apparently in the throes of a revolution. Kaiser abdicated and with the crown prince left Germany for Holland. News of armistice received comparatively quietly by the settlement.' The following day William received a letter from his brother that he would visiting Paignton and would try to visit Princetown.

Rather than have his brother come to Princetown, William decided to take a weekend's leave and walk to the coast.

'November 16th. Left settlement at 7.40 a.m. to walk to Paignton to see Wilfrid. Went across the moors by the Tor Royal road now being made by the C.O.'s. Several of our men were on the way to work and I did not envy them as there was a keen S.E. wind and they looked shrivelled up. The road to Totnes was a very pretty one, the autumn colours were in full glory and showed up well. Reached Totnes at

12.05 and Paignton at 1.20. Found Wilfrid at the shop (19 Palace Avenue) and was shown over the premises and was struck by the cleanliness and orderliness of the arrangements. Wilfrid and I took train to Torquay and had a good view of the rough seas dashing over the wall on to the train lines. At Torquay we went to the Theatre Royal and saw the play "As you Like it" performed by the Compton Comedy Co. At 7.30 we went to the Pavilion and saw "The Birth of a Nation". Stayed at the Fleet Hotel.

'November 17th. Got off after breakfast and walked round by the cliffs to Anstey's Cove, Babbacombe to Newton Abbott. Here Wilfrid caught the 4 p.m. train for Paignton whilst I started off for Princetown. Enjoyed my weekend and although there was a keen wind most of the time and scarcely a glimpse of the sun the weather was excellent for walking. Wilfrid insisted on paying all expenses.'

On November 21st, the camp were told by the Home Office that they would not be released until the soldiers had been de-mobilised. William reports several more meetings of the settlement to press for release, but little else seemed to happen. On New Year's Eve the camp was 'serenaded' by Scotsmen. There was one more visit from Wilfrid on March 29th and 30th 1919, and that is the last record in the diary.

William was released from Dartmoor in April 1919, and the settlement was returned to its original use as a prison.

On April 25th the Western Morning News reported '...*the removal of the conscientious objectors who brought the grim old prison into the limelight with their fads, their antics, and their shirking of duties as citizens...*' It concluded '...*the long haired "conchies" will soon become a mere memory of the great war- its most exasperating memory.'*

CHAPTER FIVE

BETWEEN THE WARS

L IKE MANY CONSCIENTIOUS OBJECTORS RETURNING HOME, William struggled to find work. Councils often passed resolutions refusing to employ conscientious objectors. His old job at Northampton Council was not open for him to return to. Wilfrid wrote that his brother was well qualified to take on other clerical work, *'but when references were asked for and his war record disclosed, he found himself very isolated.'*

Help came from a friend of the family. Wenman Joseph Bassett-Lowke was one of Northampton's more famous entrepreneurs. Born in 1877, the son of a Northampton boiler maker, he founded the famous toy model company that carries his name. He loved modern architecture and interior design, commissioning Charles Rennie Mackintosh to design the interior of his home at 78 Derngate. The house is now beautifully restored, a popular attraction for lovers of Mackintosh. He was, like the Church family, a pacifist, progressive in politics and non-conformist in attitudes.

During the First World War W.J. Bassett-Lowke had diversified his business by the purchase of narrow-gauge steam railways. One of those was at Fairbourne on the Welsh coast, built to support the little holiday village that had grown across the estuary from Barmouth. In

1919 he learned of William Church's difficulties on being released from Dartmoor and offered him work.

> He was 'a broadminded and sympathetic gentleman who was good enough to offer my brother employment at Fairbourne', wrote Wilfrid. 'Here Mr Bassett Lowke had a miniature railway which was for the enjoyment of the seaside visitors. My brother accepted the post of manager, ticket collector etc. It was, I believe, just the occupation necessary to counteract his lengthy spell under duress. I called to see him on occasion and at one time found him digging away the sand that the strong sea breezes had blown over the railway lines.'

In the early 1920s Bassett Lowke sold Fairbourne Railway and William returned to Northampton to live with his parents. How he earned a living from then on is not clear. He did some work for his brother- '... *at times, I was able to give him occupation in attending to my accounts*' Wilfrid wrote. '*He being wonderfully accurate and painstaking in drawing up balance sheets and clerical work generally.*'

William resumed the one great love of his life, chess. In 1920 he became captain of the Northampton league of the Chess Club and his father Wesley was secretary. By 1924 William had replaced his father as secretary, and reported to the annual general meeting that he had won the club handicap tournament, his father coming second. Father and son remained leading lights in Northampton Chess club for the rest of their lives.

In 1924 Wesley, now aged 70, found himself in a spot of bother with the authorities. He was stopped by a policeman on the Billing Road and charged with riding a bicycle on the pavement. The Northampton Police Court, chaired by the Mayor, Councillor Lewis, reported in the Daily Echo under the heading 'The Billing Road Difficulty'. '*The Defendant admitted riding the cycle on the footpath but said he did so much against his will. It was impossible to ride on the road. He only rode a very few yards.*' The nature of the obstruction blocking the pavement was not reported.

'The Mayor pointed out that there had been a number of similar cases and the magistrates were obliged to inflict a nominal fine of 2s 6d. He hoped the reasons for these appearances would very quickly disappear.'

The same session of the Police Court dealt with a man fined 10 shillings for using bad language and another fined 5 shillings for riding a bicycle at night without a light.

A growing business and family

Wilfrid and Naomi's family continued to grow. In 1920 their first son, Philip, was born followed by Wilfrid Vivian in 1923. The growing family required a larger house, so in 1922 they moved from 23 Ennerdale Rd just round the corner to 'Campbells', No. 1 The Avenue, Spinney Hill, then in 1924 to 18 Abington Park Crescent. Wilfrid and Naomi were to spend the rest of their lives in a home overlooking Abington Park.

For a couple of years after the end of the war, the business continued to grow. Annual takings rose from £5,195 in 1918 to £7,920 in 1921. From 1922 onwards turnover dropped or stood still every year throughout the rest of the 1920's and dropping further

Wilfrid and Naomi with Joy, Irene, Philip and Stumps.

89

with the recession of the early 1930's to a low of £5,512. It wasn't until the outbreak of the second world war that it returned to what it had been in 1919.

The newly acquired business in Paignton was re-named Church's China. A friend, Miss Slade, managed it for Wilfrid until she bought the business in about 1930. Wilfrid visited the shop when on holiday and exchanged stock, continuing a close association for as long as it remained under Miss Slade's control.

Despite difficult trading, Wilfrid still invested in improving his business. In 1922 he negotiated a new lease with the owners of the Emporium Arcade. The 21 years lease at a rent of £600 per year was for the ground floor and basement, together with four showrooms on the second floor. The first floor was not included, so that meant a long set of

Church's China at the entrance to the Emporium Arcade.

Advert Lift 1924.

stairs for customers to climb. In 1924 Wilfrid installed Northampton's first shop lift, providing access to these new showrooms. The lift had a fine wood panelled interior and iron cage style gates. It was installed by the local lift manufacturer Smith Major and Stevens, who later merged with Express Lifts. For many years after the demolition of the Emporium Arcade the lift occupied a corner of Abington Park Museum.

Wyndcroft

The honeymoon holiday at Penlee in 1911 had established a lifelong love of the South Devon coast. Penlee is a few miles south of Dartmouth, on a rocky promontory known as Matthew's (Matts) Point, overlooking the popular beach of Blackpool Sands, with stunning views over Start Bay.

Sometime soon after their honeymoon visit, a new house was built on the hill behind Penlee, accessible at that time only by a long flight of steep steps from the main road. Wilfrid bought this house, named Wyndcroft. It became a family holiday home for the rest of his life and is still used by his grandchildren and great grandchildren.

The family enjoyed long summer holidays there, sometimes with an additional short break in the spring, and the house was also let to others. On one occasion Wilfrid's elderly parents visited and were photographed on a nearby beach.

Wesley & Sarah Church (in a wheelchair) on a Devon beach with their maid Annie.

Three deaths

Sarah Church's arthritis had confined her to a wheelchair for several years. In 1926 she died, aged 71. The obituary in the Daily Echo paid tribute to a lifetime's work for the temperance movement, including the position of vice-president of the Northampton branch of the British Women's Total Abstinence Union, whose members attended her funeral. Members of Northampton Women's Own, of which she was a former president were there too.

Wesley continued to live at Holly Road with his unmarried son and daughter, William and Dora. He died on 15th April 1929 aged seventy-five. His obituary in the Northampton Daily Echo referred to his early involvement with the YMCA, and to 'becoming prominent as a teacher of music and shorthand.' It correctly pointed out that his main interest was chess; he had recently been made a life member of the Northampton chess club. The article also records that he won chess matches in simultaneous games (one player playing several games at the same time with several opponents) against famous chess players J.H. Blackburn, Boris Kostic and Sir George Thomas. His involvement in College St. Baptist Church and his role as a director of Northampton Temperance Hall were also mentioned.

> *'Mr Church was devoted to cycling and up to the last he scorned the motor car. On one occasion he rode a tricycle from Bournemouth to Northampton and had many excursions on the penny farthing type of bicycle. He was also one of the first cyclists in the town to ride on pneumatic tyres.'*

The funeral at College St Baptist Church was simple: *'dismal black as Mr Church styled it – was not to be worn by the followers'* reported The Echo. It was well attended. As well as his family, there were representatives from all the organisations with whom he'd played a prominent role: The Temperance movement, the Rechabites, the Chess Club, the YMCA, together with the staff of Church's China.

William Church (left) at a chess tournament in 1934,
a few weeks before he died.

With both their parents dead, William and his sister Dora now moved to 15 Church Way, Weston Favell. William continued to play a prominent role in Northampton Chess Club. In 1932 he won the club championship once again and on 3rd March 1934 there was a rare picture of him playing in a chess tournament. Three months later, aged 54, he was dead.

William died suddenly at home on 27th May 1934. The death certificate records that his brother, Wilfrid, was with him. The reason for his death is given as both Ascites and Bandi's disease. Ascites is the abnormal accumulation of fluid in the abdominal cavity, commonly associated with cirrhosis of the liver. Bandi may be a mis-spelling of banti's syndrome, a relatively rare disease involving the enlargement of the spleen, frequently associated with ascites, jaundice and internal bleeding. If this was the reason for William's death, he is likely to have been ill for some considerable time. In his wartime diaries there are a couple of references to stomach pains and gastric illnesses. Whether it was his extreme walking exercises, his treatment in prison and work camps or his vegetarian diet that contributed to his early death is unknown.

The Mercury and Herald report headlined 'Death of Mr W.W. Church Brilliant Chess Player' noted both his walking and chess pursuits:

'Few men in the Midlands can have tramped as many miles as Mr Church has done in amazingly short times. His greatest feat was to walk from Southampton to Northampton, a distance of approximately 104 miles, in 24 ½ hours.

'Mr Church was a brilliant chess player and he entered the national competitions on more than one occasion.'

There was not a word written about his wartime conscientious objection, his time in prison or the Dyce and Dartmoor work camps. All of that was left unreported.

In September 1934 the Northampton Chess Club announced that, in William's honour, it would buy a trophy, to be known as the 'Church

Cup'. This would be presented to the winner of an annual handicap tournament. The cup still exists today in the chess club's collection.

Wilfrid described his brother as 'odd', just as he had described himself in letters to Naomi. William was doubtless an introvert, but that does not mean that he was shy. He had a huge range of interests including music, politics and philosophy. Despite only a basic education, he read widely and developed strong principles for which he was prepared to sacrifice his liberty, his career, and his social status.

The scars of the first world war were still keenly felt in 1934, along with continued resentment towards those who refused to fight and had survived. Looking back on his life one hundred years later, his stand against war on a point of principle does not seem like something we should quietly forget. It was a key part of his life for which he should bear no shame.

Wilfrid Church's diary

With the loss of both his parents and his brother, Wilfrid was now left with Naomi and their four children and two unmarried sisters. Dora continued to live at Weston Favell and worked in the family business. Hilda, working as a hospital almoner (a form of social worker), moved first to London and later to Pevensey near Eastbourne. There was no wider Church family, only some distant cousins through Wilfrid's mother's family, with whom he had little contact. Naomi was close to her many sisters; she visited them regularly, and they became the focus of the extended family.

Wilfrid Church

After William's death, Wilfrid found his diaries. He wrote: '*He left behind him a small bundle of diaries which came into my possession* and were put aside for some years. Occasionally I would pick them up and endeavour to find something of family or other interest.' Maybe they inspired him to write his own diary, he started it just a year after William died.

Wilfrid's diaries provide the main resource for the rest of this book. They survive mostly in hardback notebooks, handwritten, with one book per year from 1935 right through to a few weeks before his death in 1973. They start with quite short entries, but after a year or so they become longer, with single entries sometimes extending over several pages.

Wilfrid certainly intended that the diaries would be private during his lifetime, but he was aware that in time other people would read them. Some notes he wrote in old age act as an introduction to the diaries and explain their purpose.

'It may be just as well though to keep the diary in a private drawer or perhaps in a modern safe so that prying eyes do not find references which they might find a ghoulish pleasure in divulging at just that opportune moment. References to irksome and fussy relations make it important for the diary to be placed well out of their way.'

'Much could be said about the wisdom or harm done by making entries and storing them like pots of jam away in some dark corner. Preservation may lead to sourness, mould, an undesirable atmosphere etc. "The evil that man does lives after him". But the disclosures may at times be sweet memories, helpful and pleasantly sentimental with a passing thought or two of the good old days.'

The diaries contain many personal remarks and criticisms, particularly of members of his family which were clearly intended to be private. Out of respect to Wilfrid and the people concerned they will not appear in this book.

Like his brother, Wilfrid often recorded precise details of journeys with routes and times. He wrote about his holidays, gardening, beekeeping, the weather, the theatre and just about anything else he was doing. In total they provide a complete picture of a middle aged, middle class man and his family in the middle of the 20th century, but they also give a personal insight into the political upheavals of the time, and their consequences for Wilfrid and his family. He thought about how his diaries may have a historical interest. In 1937 he wrote that he had been listening on the radio to a talk by Lord Ponsonby entitled 'British diarists' which dealt particularly with diarists of the 17th century. *'He spoke of not only the historic value of these writings but also how they threw light on the manners and customs of long ago. Am inspired by this talk to make of this diary something more interesting than of late'*

The diary starts inconsequentially on 21st March 1935 with Wilfrid and Naomi taking a day trip to Nottingham, stopping at Oakham on the way for Naomi to recall her time working there 28 years earlier. The day finished with an evening visit to the 'Rep' (Northampton Repertory Theatre) for a performance of 'For the Love of Mike', which Wilfrid thought was amateurish. A day out, visiting or sightseeing, followed by an evening at the theatre is a typical day's leisure recorded in the diary.

The family in the 1930's

A great deal of the diary is taken up with the activities of his four children, with comment on their work, their relationships, and their letters home.

When Wilfrid's diary begins, his eldest daughter Joy, aged twenty-one, is completing a course in health care in London, and is looking for further training opportunities. In April she was invited to spend two weeks 'insight training' at Woollett Hall in Kent. On 5th May 1935 Wilfrid and Naomi are rather shocked to learn that Joy had developed a relationship with the proprietor of this residential home for specialist health treatments. Leslie Korth was 48, 27 years older than Joy. However, the relationship was to last. Joy and Leslie were married in the autumn and before the end of the decade they were to have two daughters. Christine was born in 1936 and Rosalind in 1938. In 1939 Woollett Hall was sold and Leslie moved his business to Tunbridge Wells. He became president of the Nature Cure Association.

Nineteen-year-old Irene is working in London for a building society. She would develop a relationship with George Wickham, who Wilfrid and Naomi felt did not have the income to support the lifestyle Irene would expect. They became engaged, but in January 1939 the engagement was called off.

The eldest son, Philip, is fifteen in 1935. He would finish school and join the family business in 1937. Attempts for Phil to get more training and experience in business were not very successful. He didn't enjoy evening classes in book-keeping at the local college, and several months doing work experience with a china and glass retailer in Birmingham were not successful. In 1939 he joined the Royal Air Force Reserve. A few days before the outbreak of war, he received his conscription papers for full time service in the RAF.

Vivian (Wilfrid is his first name, but not used) is twelve when the diary begins. He is at the grammar school, his passion for fishing already well identified by his parents. Writing home from a holiday in Germany a few years earlier, Wilfrid said Viv, who was only seven at the time, would have loved watching the fish in a pond in their hotel courtyard.

In September 1936, Viv, together with Stephen Dickens and Noel Beattie were caught by a policeman in the act of the heinous crime of gathering conkers in Abington Park. Mrs Dickens, their next-door neighbour had provided a ladder to help the boys, but broken branches meant an interview with the Chief Constable. Later, Wilfrid identified his youngest son's interest in the countryside and the outdoor environment and wondered if he might take up a career in forestry.

Wilfrid and Naomi regularly visited Naomi's many sisters and their families in Cambridge. Less often the sisters came to visit Northampton. As many of them were much older that Naomi, they had several children who were only a few years younger than Naomi and they became friends. These included Elliott Ridgeon, the son of Naomi's sister Beatrice, who joined his father's successful Cambridge timber merchant business.

The Rotary Club

The Rotary Club had been founded in Northampton in 1921. Wilfrid isn't listed as one of the founding members, but by the time he started writing his diary he was an established member. He frequently recorded the topic of the weekly talk. These posed questions such as 'Is profit making a satisfactory motive for business?' or 'The need for practical psychology in education'. They also covered figures from the arts or politics, such as Handel and Kier Hardie.

In response to one debate, in February 1936, entitled 'Is restriction in the use of new inventions becoming necessary?', Wilfrid wrote several pages. He referred to Bassett-Lowke 'not quite so electric as usual' quoting 'Saint Bernard Shaw'. Shaw had stayed at Basett-Lowke's home at 78 Derngate. In 1939 Bassett-Lowke gave a cine film presentation on his trip to the West Indies.

In 1937 Wilfrid was elected to the Rotary Council. As his involvement with Rotary grew, he attended weekend conferences, often with Naomi, to Buxton, Blackpool and Skegness. He wasn't used to formal events. The reception with the Mayor and Mayoress of Buxton was the first time he had worn a dress suit. *'Of course our dancing is not very accurate but we enjoyed the experience'* he wrote.

Three Kings

Naomi keenly followed royal events, Wilfrid took an interest too, but not with quite the same enthusiasm. On January 20th 1936 they heard the news bulletin 'The King's life is moving peacefully towards its close'. The previous year they had attended the silver jubilee celebrations of George V, and on 28th January they were off to London to see his funeral. *'It was a wonderful sight'* wrote Wilfrid *'King Edward VIII was plainly seen by us and the various famous personalities seem to pass by in endless formation. It is quite possible that never before has such a procession been seen in London.'*

In November 1936 he attended a meeting at the Guildhall to discuss the planning for Edward VIII's coronation celebrations. He joined the decorations committee but a month later they discovered that it wouldn't be Edward VIII's coronation after all, but George VI's. Royal occasions were important to the china and glass retailer, but Wilfrid now had the wrong stock. *'Now that the King has abdicated, I am left with two or three hundred pieces of 'Coronation' articles'* he wrote.

In February 1937 he attended a meeting of the decorations committee to receive tenders, but in his view the committee didn't have the budget they needed. *'The town have only allowed us £25 towards the expenses but we are loath to proceed unless the town advance at least £100.'* He doesn't mention the matter again, so it isn't clear if more money was found.

On Coronation Day, 12th May, Naomi was disappointed that Wilfrid did not take her to London to see the parade for herself. Wilfrid confides in his diary that *'her disappointment has given him discomfort'.* Instead they attended an open-air service on Northampton Market Square and watched a fleet of lorries depicting 'tableaux' of Northampton's historic events. They then listened to the coronation on the radio. *'To have been in the abbey itself would have been the happening of a lifetime,'* wrote Wilfrid *'but to hear the ritual on the wireless was rather a depressing ordeal. Perhaps I am wrong in writing this, but on a dull day the chanting, the responses, and the words that cannot all be translated or understood are apt to cause a slightly depressed person still deeper moroseness.'*

The day ended with a downpour that forced the public firework show to be cancelled, a cheery Wilfrid concluded: *'And so ends Coronation Day, a day in which neither M. nor I have been very socially disposed to each other.'*

The next day Naomi took Viv and a friend to London to see the decorations. They joined a crowd outside Buckingham Palace and saw the new king and queen wave from the balcony. Wilfrid stayed behind, helping with a tour organised by the Chamber of Trade to view the decorations in nearby towns. Thirty cars set out carrying passengers who were charged 3s/6d with the proceeds going to the General Hospital. *'The decorations at Kettering and Wellingborough were very ordinary but the effort at Bedford was indeed a praiseworthy one'* concluded Wilfrid.

Bees

Wilfrid frequently reported on his beekeeping efforts. Beehives were kept in the garden and on the garage roof, requiring considerable attention at certain times of the year, particularly when swarming. Wilfrid was frequently seeking out swarms in the neighbours' gardens or getting help and advice from a local beekeeping expert, Mr Swann. On 5th August 1937 he reports in full one incident which disturbed a sultry suburban summer's day.

'Scene. Abington Park Crescent in the vicinity of No. 18. Phil, Sweeting and Peter Andrews about to obtain their bicycles from in front of no. 18. John Andrews in his young lady's Morris car outside No. 19 [The Andrews family were next door neighbours]. *A gas man with ladder about to clean the glass of a gas standard lamp on the other side of the road. A workman proceeding from No. 16 with his can in which he is accustomed to make tea. He is proceeding towards No 18 for the aforesaid ritual. The father of Mrs Andrews is peacefully sitting in the garden of No. 19.*

'M. [Naomi] *is just finishing the washing up after a mid-day meal, the windows are pleasantly open as there is a sultry atmosphere, thunder being expected. Time 2.15pm. I ascend the ladder and reach the garage roof with the usual equipment for*

subduing the bees, namely smokers, carbolic cloths, knife to prize open the supers and of course veil and gloves. I however took a chance and wore only low shoes. I should have puffed smoke in the entrance of the hive before dissembling the parts. This with my low shoes was mistake number two. Having taken off lifts I prize off all the supers together but find they are particularly heavy; in fact they are as much as I can carry. The bees immediately proceed to emit angry noises to show the acutest displeasure rising up rapidly, swooping down vindictively and with marvellous accuracy finding out my vulnerable parts which were my ankles. They came at my poorly protected quarters of my anatomy in scores and the stings inflicted were countless. I did not stop to complete my work but waving the smokers about at my veil and mainly at my ankles I beat a retreat down the ladder and into the garage with hundreds of bees in pursuit. It was indeed a painful experience but fortunately except for two stings under my chin the dire work was concentrated round both ankles causing them great pain and ultimately much swelling.

'In the meantime, the three lads afore mentioned were quickly driven from their efforts to reach their cycles. Sweeting was stung once, Peter Andrews received two, one of which was obtained by a bee becoming entangled in his hair. Says Peter 'get this bee out of my hair Phil' but upon looking round Peter saw Phil running with unbelievable speed up the Crescent and almost out of sight. John Andrews with the car was highly amused at this interlude until some bees caught sight of him too and inflicted three choice stings upon his person. He made a rapid retreat, but this hero departed by car. The workman with the can, considering things looked dangerous and having received one sting only, turned his back on the scene and with lurid language went towards the scene of his labours.

'The uniformed gas lamp cleaner heard bees rushing around his person and he was seen up the ladder waving his arms and hat about. He too is said to have expressed himself forcibly. M. who should of course have been safe indoors, and no doubt would have *escaped had she been the usual person and kept more windows closed, found a disagreeable bee on her nose inserting her sting there. M. was distinctly angry with the undignified attack.*

'The father of Mrs Andrews discovered that 'the fly in the ointment' of a garden was in this instance a bee and unfortunately he received a sample sting. It was quite a hectic afternoon.'

Theatre

Wilfrid and Naomi attended the theatre or cinema weekly, sometimes with a second visit. Their regular destination was Northampton Repertory Theatre 'The Rep', now known as The Royal Theatre in Guildhall Rd. Less often, they attended the New Theatre in Abington Street, which was better known for more popular entertainment.

In one of his few references to the cinema, Wilfrid described the classic film 'Anna Karenina' starring Greta Garbo, shown at the Northampton Plaza in May 1936, as *rather a disappointing film*. He preferred a play at The Rep called 'Service', which he saw that evening.

Frequently, his involvement in the Rotary club, his interest in the theatre and his political interests happily came together. In October 1938 the Rotary club were invited to the Rep to see a performance of 'The Insect Play'. *'This is a weird and fanciful production and is supposed to be peace propaganda'* wrote Wilfrid *'I fear it would be rather misunderstood and not greatly appreciated.'* Despite that he thought the play 'was a remarkably good effort' and he was pleased that many Rotarians and their wives were present.

Friends frequently invited Wilfrid and Naomi to the theatre. On one occasion Mr Bassett-Lowke, who was a director of the Royal Theatre, invited them to a gathering of 'helpers' at the County Café. Afterwards he gave them seats at a performance of 'Sally Who?' at the Rep. His comment *'I rather regret to state my feelings in the company of Labourites were rather out of harmony. Perhaps I was rather a stranger to them'* suggests that this was a favour to political helpers of Bassett-Lowke, who was a Labour councillor.

In March 1937 Wilfrid's brother-in-law, Cyril Ridgeon, invited him to Cambridge Rotary Club to hear Dame Sybil Thorndike and her husband Lewis Casson. She talked about 'some aspects of the service of the Theatre to the Community.' The famous actor talked about how the behaviour of an audience impacted upon the cast, reminiscing with stories to make her point. The theatre's object, said Dame Sybil, was to get audiences to understand other human beings and to see through other peoples' eyes and to stand in the shoes of different individuals.

In the evening Wilfrid, Naomi, Cyril and some of Naomi's sisters saw Sybil and her husband performing in 'Six men of Dorset', a play based on the story of the Tolpuddle Martyrs. Sybil Thorndike's radical sympathies doubtless lay behind this choice of play, and afterwards she spoke about it. *'There were conditions even now which call for redress and she besought the youth to champion the downtrodden'*. Wilfrid wrote, *'The acting of course was splendid, and it is good to realise that this play is being produced with a purpose.'* However, *'Auntie Trix* [Naomi's sister Beatrice] *and Cyril do not appreciate the play.'*

Six months later they saw Dame Sybil Thorndike again, this time in Northampton at the New Theatre, in a play called 'Yes My Darling Daughter'. The play, which dealt with sexual freedom, was clearly not to Wilfrid's taste *'Both M and I were rather surprised that S. Thorndike should have appeared in this type of* play.'

Wilfrid seemed to enjoy his own private theatrical and musical criticism. One evening in 1937 he was up late at night with Naomi listening to the wireless.

'As I write this at 11.30pm Verdi's Otello is being broadcast from the Covent Garden Opera House. All I hope is that the actual audience is enjoying this more than I.' Naomi wanted to listen to it because it was thought to be 'high class' *'but had my own tastes been consulted and I had had my choice I should have preferred some real bad dance music.'*

'This Verdi opera is in a foreign language, the plot is downright horrible and the singing, to my mind, is mostly interspersed with

shrieks and howls. … My private opinion (of course not to be disclosed) is: Something awful couldn't be worse, throat splitting and horrible, real bad taste, useless as an inspiration and only fit for snobs and the callous aristocracy to listen to.'

Wilfrid also confided to his diary on several occasions that he was no fan of Shakespeare. He commended a performance of Romeo and Juliet at The Rep in 1938 but added *'Must confess to no great liking for Shakespeare plays'*. His tastes changed though; during the war he read Shakespeare plays and copied large chunks of verse into the back of one of his diaries.

Healthy living

Wilfrid continued his interest in healthy living, particularly vegetarianism.

He wrote about his usual morning routine *'Down about 8 in the morning after the usual rituals in the bathroom, then letting Jock* [The Airedale Terrier] *out and entering the garage to get the worn-out skipping rope. Then the usual hundred skips, after which the preparation of ripe fruit for breakfast.'*

He worried about modern diets, and he was disappointed that his family were not keeping to his dietary principles. After Vivian had a tooth removed he wrote *'This evening feeling perhaps a little overwrought I rather let myself go and in the presence of Florrie* [the maid], *who was in the kitchen, complained of the manner in which the children were fed, blaming milk that was sugared, soft foods and lack of hard foods for the sorry state into which the teeth of the two lads had arrived. … The difficulty there is in persuading the young to stand firm against the tempting dainties, sweets and condiments that are as attractive to them as sugar is to flies.'* He said to Naomi, Phil and Florrie *'Have what you like, do not consider me, cook your meat or fish and I will be mum. And so this evening I have felt a deep disappointment.'*

Wilfrid was President of the Northampton branch of the British Union for the Abolition of Vivisection. About 100 people attended a meeting in July 1937 in the Market Square. Another meeting in 1939 failed to attract so much interest. A guest speaker *'spoke to empty cars and bare stones'*. A speaker against vivisection at the Rotary Club meeting in April 1936, failed to convince club members, who asked for another speaker to make the alternative case.

There was a similar disappointment for the Vegetarian Society. Wilfrid hosted a meeting in his home in February 1936 with a talk given on 'humanitarianism'. *'About eighteen present and the discussion was not too brilliant. The vegetarian efforts are somewhat depressing.'* He wasn't discouraged, in 1940 the Chronicle and Echo reported a talk he gave to Northampton Rotary Club. His case for vegetarianism was based primarily on healthy eating, but also upon an ethical opposition to killing animals. Modern environmentalists would share his claim that a vegetarian economy would mean a more efficient use of the land. Bassett-Lowke deflated Wilfrid's argument that vegetarianism leads to more peaceful attitudes by pointing out that Hitler, Stalin and Mussolini were all vegetarians. The response from Wilfrid was that their diets gave them energy that was put in the wrong directions.

Wilfrid enjoyed walking, not the extreme speed and long-distance walking of his brother but a good Sunday walk out into Northamptonshire countryside with his dog, an Airedale terrier called Jock. During the summer both Wilfrid and Naomi enjoyed tennis, contributing to a lifestyle which kept them both fit. In 1940 Wilfrid records his weight as being 9st 2lb.

In addition to at least two trips a year to Wyndcroft, there were other short holidays around the country. North Wales was a favourite destination, particularly Arthog on the Mawddach estuary, very close to where his brother William used to work on the Fairbourne railway. Other destinations were Llanfachreth near Dolgellau and Dolwyddelan near Bettws y Coed. Vegetarianism also contributed to their holidays. In June 1937 Wilfrid and Naomi spent a long weekend with three of Naomi's sisters and their husbands at a 'food reform establishment' at Branksome Dene near Bournemouth.

There were out of season walking holidays without Naomi, but with two friends Harry Cooper and Tom Braybrooke, to North Wales, The Malvern hills and to Devon.

There were three overseas holidays during this pre-war period. In the late 1920's Wilfrid and Joy went on a walking holiday in Corsica. In 1930 Wilfrid and Naomi went on a holiday fellowship trip to Germany, cruising on the Rhine and visiting Cologne, Marburg, Frankfurt and Munich. The climax of the holiday was a visit to Oberammergau to see the alpine town's famous passion play. A year before the war started there was a trip to Norway on the cruise ship 'The Atlantis'. W.J. Bassett-Lowke had organised a group of Northampton people to join the cruise departing from Tilbury docks, sailing across the North Sea and up the Fjord coast.

The storm clouds gather

Unlike in 1914, the prospect of war in the late 1930's was no surprise. Wilfrid's diary doesn't often refer to current political affairs, but when it does, it is to share his worries at the prospect of war.

On 6th January 1936, Northampton Rotary club debated 'Is preparation for war likely to ensure peace?' That this was the topic for debate indicates unease for the future, but Wilfrid just expressed frustration that his remarks fell flat and that he '*had some difficulty in linking up my points.*' Later in the year while on holiday in Devon he attended a meeting of Paignton Rotary Club, addressed by the local MP Major Raynor. '*Needless to say, he is a Conservative*' wrote Wilfrid. '*His talk on the European situation was rather disjointed but the main theme seemed to be our unreadiness in the event of war. He said our position was ten or twenty times worse than in 1914 and that the state of affairs at present were perfectly bloody.*'

Never short on curiosity, Wilfrid and Naomi attended a public meeting at Northampton Guildhall on in November 1936 addressed by

Sir Oswald Mosley. The Northampton Chronicle and Echo reported:

> *'Friendship with Germany and Italy at the sacrifice of Russia; a bargain with Japan, which would give that country a free hand in north China; and non-intervention in Spain were advocated as the ways to world peace by Sir Oswald Mosley at a fascist meeting at Northampton Town Hall.*
>
> *'Standing in Front of a Union Jack Sir Oswald addressed a crowded audience, which filled all balconies and most of the standing room downstairs.'*

Wilfrid's record of the meeting was brief: *'He came to the platform unintroduced and spoke without any serious interruption for over an hour'* he wrote. *'There were about fifty 'blackshirts' lining the hall in anticipation of disorder. Sir O.M. is quite a good speaker, his attitude is not that of the pacifist and he has the manner of the disciple of the 'mailed fist'.*

A year later Wilfrid attended another large meeting on the threat of war with his sister-in-law Ada Mowl. The meeting, in November 1937 in the Repertory Theatre, was addressed by Laurence Housman and Rev. Henry Carter. As a playwright, Housman shared Wilfrid's love of the theatre. He was a pacifist, a socialist, and had actively supported women's suffrage.

The Northampton Mercury reported that Housman *'accused Britain and the allies of nullifying the idea of a war-to-end-war by imposing a war minded peace on the vanquished, notably Germany, by the treaty of Versailles.'* Mr Housman said *'they had lost the peace because when the war was over, they remained war minded. If they had been peace-minded at Versailles things would not have been so.'* Wilfrid wrote, *'they were two excellent speakers, both keen out-and-out pacifists.'*

Another meeting attended by Wilfrid was organised by the Northampton Left Book Club. Mr Harry Pollitt from the Communist Party was the main speaker, together with Reginald Paget, Labour's prospective candidate and future MP for Northampton. *'Mr Pollitt gave an enthusiastic speech on the dangers of fascism to world peace,'* wrote Wilfrid. *'This meeting made one think that the world is full of wrongs, that there is an abundance to put right, that we are hopeless as human beings and that the clouds of evil roll relentlessly over us. I am looking for a rainbow.'*

As the threat of war grew, so did the preparations. In January 1938 Wilfrid wrote *'I have been debating in my mind whether to register under the Air Raid Precautions Scheme or not.'* He had already been approached and was expecting another call. *'Have decided against taking up this call'* he concluded *'not so much because it appears to be against any principles I may have but because I feel rather suspicious of its workings. It would of course be much saner to combat the cause of war rather than prepare to minimise the effects of destruction.'*

Only a day later he had changed his mind. *'...after all my cogitations I have decided to support the scheme and this evening I accordingly signed the papers.'* He went on to say that his wife and sons had swayed him, *'as it did not violate any of my anti-war principles.'*

On 20th September 1938 Wilfrid attended his first Air Raid Precautions (ARP) training session. *'I take it not to be a military association but the attaining of some knowledge necessary to safeguard human beings from the devastation of a mad world'* wrote Wilfrid. The topic was dealing with poison gas. *'Whether it is through the blare and stunt of the newspapers I do not know but the thought of war seems to be sinking more and more deeply into the minds of people. Am hoping that we may be able to trust our leaders to guide us safely through these disturbing times.'*

The tension over Czechoslovakia was weighing on Wilfrid. On 27th September he went to Cedar Road School to pick up a supply of gas masks, but they had already been snapped up. The following day headlines in the newspapers that 'every man and woman must act' must have reminded him of the early days of the previous war. He now had a stock of gas masks and distributed them in Abington Park Crescent.

On 29th September, the news was better. We look on the Munich agreement differently now, but as Chamberlain declared 'peace in our time' Wilfrid was far from alone in celebrating. *'Great relief is felt throughout the country of the good news of a settlement of the Czech trouble. Chamberlain has evidently done well and now we hope that in future more attention will be paid to the efficacy of conferences.'*

Despite some relief in the tension, the Air Raid Precaution classes continued. Wilfrid recognised the need to prepare for the consequences of war. *'They broach a horrible subject and I am not sure but that in the minds of some people the idea of attack by a foreign nation is not fostered by these meetings.'*

In March 1939, Wilfrid commented about the German invasion of Czechoslovakia. *'Germany has been accused of robbing the Czechoslovakians of their country. Certainly, we live dangerously on the edge of arsenals and one dare hardly let the imagination roam.'*

Philip Church returned from his work experience in Birmingham with a view to developing the wholesale side of Church's China. On 1st April he discussed with his pacifist father joining the RAF reserve as a volunteer. Wilfrid confided in his diary that he opposed the 'military spirit' and that made it difficult for him to give advice to his son. The Chamberlain government was legislating to re-introduce conscription, so Wilfrid knew that his sons were likely to end up in military service in any case. Wilfrid signed the relevant forms for Phil to volunteer and made the following entry in his diary. *'It has caused me much thought and anxiety, but as he has apparently no scruples about the step and as I do not commit myself by appending my signature there seems no other thing to do but accept the fact.'*

On 28th April, Wilfrid heard a broadcast of a speech by Hitler to the German Reichstag. The speech is in response to a request from President Roosevelt to respect the territorial integrity of a long list of countries in Europe and further afield. Hitler replied by renouncing the Anglo-German naval pact and the German-Polish non-aggression pact. He offered to negotiate new non-aggression pacts with any nation that asked for them. Perhaps it was this last part that led to Wilfrid's surprising entry in his diary.

'Today Hitler's speech has been broadcast. His utterances were not too violent, and I thought them to be well reasoned and controlled. The general comment of the press is unfairly critical and although I am not unmindful of the German apparent hardness, yet I consider some respect or even commendation should be expressed on his statements. It seems that a warlike spirit is seething in our nation, but I trust the heat will not burst into flame.'

If Wilfrid had heard or seen the speech being delivered it is hard to believe that he would have thought the words were reasoned or controlled. Film footage shows Hitler, surrounded by uniformed Nazis reciting in an exaggerated, sarcastic and dismissive manner the list of 31 countries on which Roosevelt was seeking assurances. The speech was interspersed with laughs and cheers from the Reichstag and followed by lengthy footage of military parades. It was hardly to Wilfrid's taste. Doubtless he was trying to see through the warmongering propaganda in the English press. That and a naïve wish that war could be averted may have coloured his opinion.

Philip was sworn into the RAF reserve on 25th May. This meant fortnightly attendance at Sywell aerodrome and two weeks training a year, plus evening classes.

Refugees and Evacuees

On 29th July a Jewish refugee boy came to stay at the Church family home. Walter Sulke was sixteen years old. He had been at Bunce Court, a private school at Otterden, near Faversham in Kent. The school had been founded in Germany in 1926. It moved to the UK in 1933 after the Nazis took power. The school's pupils were predominantly Jewish due to the difficulty their parents had found in finding school places for their children in Germany. It operated on Montessori principles, with a strong emphasis on outdoor activities and healthy living that would have been attractive to Wilfrid.

Walter Sulke *'was a very intelligent and nice lad'* was Wilfrid's first reaction. *'He believes in the inevitability of war, but perhaps that has been impressed on his mind by the military character of the German people.'*

A longer talk with Walter on a walk in the grounds of Castle Ashby led to Wilfrid forming a more negative opinion. *'His outlook seems rather fatalistic and he speaks of an early war with Germany as inevitable and a war, he says, that would have Germany victorious in about three weeks.'* Wilfrid thought this was due to being brought up in Germany and taught to use a machine gun at the age of twelve. *'... his outlook seems to be woefully warlike, much company of this type of person is apt to bring depression and lessen one's faith in the good intentions of our neighbours.'* By the time Walter left, Wilfrid had learned that he came from Berlin. His father had just been imprisoned and his mother was in Hungary.

Irene, recently separated from her partner of three years, had been planning to take Vivian on holiday with her to Switzerland. With the threat of war looming, their holiday was cancelled at the last minute, and they went to Ireland instead.

A return from a short visit to Tunbridge Wells on 1st September really brought the looming crisis home: *'We make our departure from Tunbridge Wells and as we approach Reigate and the vicinity of London we see signs of crisis, children being grouped together with their small bundles and gas masks awaiting the boarding of buses and other methods of transport...'.* *'When we arrived, we found Phil had his calling up papers. This news gave us an unpleasant shock and we both felt very disturbed. I feel so strongly the futility of war and I have seen so much of the results of the last war that I am full of fear and helplessness.'*

The question of evacuees was now looming in the minds of the Rotary Club. They discussed the topic at a meeting on 28th August. On 2nd September the first of thousands of evacuees arrived in Northampton.

On Sunday morning 3rd September Wilfrid and Naomi attended Abington Avenue Congregational Church (now the United Reformed

Church), knowing that, unless Hitler responded by 11am to Chamberlain's ultimatum to withdraw German troops from Poland, then Britain would be in a state of war.

> 'At this fateful hour we were in chapel, and when we came out and made our way down the Wellingborough Rd to Bullemier's paper shop and saw that war had been declared we were indeed very depressed. Sandbags were being placed at various places and an unusual number of women and children were in evidence.' …
> 'I have spent some hours today obscuring windows.'

The four years of anguish over the prospect of another great war turned out to be justified.

CHAPTER SIX

ANOTHER WAR

'We Think too much and feel too little.
More than machinery we need humanity'.

WILFRID COPIED THESE WORDS FROM CHARLIE CHAPLIN'S FILM 'The Great Dictator' into his diary after he saw the famous film early in the war. *'An outstanding production',* wrote Wilfrid *'in which Charlie Chaplin comes into the limelight again and plays a very strong part as a dictator. It is spoken of as a brilliant satirical commentary on dictatorship.'*

He went to see the film twice. The closing speech, with its appeal to end militarism and to seek a kinder more gentle world summed up Wilfrid's thoughts on the war and are reflected time and again in the diaries.

The Phoney War

War brings sudden changes. For children, new routines create excitement, even, to begin with, fun. Blackouts, sandbags, air raid warnings, gas masks, without a bomb in sight. In September 1939 all these things were very quickly in place, but apart from that, not very much happened. The novelty soon wore off and with no sign of war activity the civil precautions soon become tiresome.

The first air raid warning was just two days after war was declared. 'About 2.45 this morning sirens, buzzers etc were giving an air raid warning' wrote Wilfrid. 'Looking from our windows the evacuees and others could be seen making their way into the park and slowly moving in groups across the dew laden grass. It was not very long before the 'all clear' signal was given and then we all resumed our normal occupations.'

The blackout quickly became an inconvenience. A twice daily chore to deal with the shutters on every window of the house.

'When windows have to be so fitted that no light is emitted it is then that one is surprised at the amount and number of windows in a house, especially our dwelling. Then too at the same time as light is kept in there is a danger of fresh air being kept out. Looking across the park at night it is noticed how well instructions have been observed, there are the outlines of trees and on a lighter night the silhouette of houses, but no glimmer of light anywhere except on a clear night the stars, which appear all the brighter on account of the contrast.'

Walking around the town at night became harder, Wilfrid wrote of walking home from the theatre one night, groping along to avoid lamp posts. Even bus windows were darkened by a blue stain on the glass and the interior lights were dimmed.

The impact on the business was felt very quickly, not on sales but on costs. 'As happened during the last war the prices of commodities are rising fast. The compulsory insurances and shortage of raw materials etc have compelled manufacturers and others to protect themselves. I am expecting my goods to be subject to a 10% rise, and should hostilities continue there is a further 10% predicted before Xmas.' Wilfrid had to insure his own stock at £6 per £100 worth.

The biggest impact of the outbreak of war was the arrival of evacuees. Plans had been in place for some months; Northampton was viewed as being safer than London and other major cities and ports. So, the town was ready to receive 39,000 evacuees at Northampton's Castle Station.

'*Northampton was due to receive its first evacuees at 12.21 today*', announced the Northampton Mercury on 1st September 1939. '*At the rate of two an hour further train loads are arriving up to 7 p.m. ... The children will be in groups of 50, each group in the charge of a teacher. There will be no hand picking of children- selection of children for homes of the type from which they come.*'

The Church household welcomed two young evacuees, Brian and Louise Appleton, aged 15 and 17. Wilfrid considered that he and Naomi were lucky to have two such well-behaved young people. Many others complained of difficulties with evacuee children from very different backgrounds to their own, torn away from their family and friends and put in a strange place with people they didn't know.

The host families of evacuee children were all paid 8s/6d per child per week, not enough to meet their needs. Wilfrid wrote to their father asking for an addition of 10s each to this state contribution. Mr Appleton replied that he was expected to reimburse the government, and as his business had been closed by the war, he couldn't afford it. However, once he could put his finances in order, he would pay. A week later Wilfrid received a £5 cheque, but Mr Appleton found somewhere else for his children to live. Many evacuees did not stay in the town for long, either they found alternative accommodation with their families, or they simply drifted back home, as at this stage in the war there was no sign of bombs. On 28th October the Appleton children departed to a cottage in Tetbury, Gloucestershire.

A son in uniform

Philip Church was the first member of Church family for generations to join the forces. On 26th November, on his first leave since receiving his call up papers, he attended chapel with his parents.

> 'Mother was naturally very proud to have tall Phil with her, a uniformed RAF sergt. And I also felt somewhat moved but should find it difficult to define my feelings. Under the influence of a sacred building and in such an atmosphere of worship serious thoughts surge, and the presence of Phil representing youth preparing to face danger filled me with foreboding and sadness.'

Philip had formed a relationship with a 'fair haired young lady' by the name of Eunice Burrows, whose family lived in Duston. He was told that he was being posted to Hastings for further training. He faced a dilemma over a request by the RAF that he be vaccinated. Vaccinations that required testing on animals were opposed by the anti-vivisection society, of which his father was a longstanding member. He shared his father's objections but agreed to the injections rather than be debarred from work for the RAF. Wilfrid's check with the anti-vivisection society confirmed that the inoculations are not supposed to be compulsory in the forces, but as Wilfrid said, 'they have a way...'

On the 2nd December Philip left for Hastings, leaving behind his apprehensive parents and the maid Florrie. 'I wonder how Florrie feels about the departure of Phil her idol' wrote Wilfrid. Leaving his son with his colleagues, he added 'I see other RAF sergeants collecting together with kit, all seemed of a healthy and happy type evidently delighting in their own company and looking forward to showing other units in Hastings what fine fellows have arrived from Northampton. ... Endeavouring to assume cheerfulness I shook hands and left him carrying his two kit bags up the drive...'.

Philip was not gone for long; he was back for Christmas. The Burrows family were invited for tea on Christmas day, and after a good season's trading at the shop, the war seemed to be far away.

The war turns real

Suddenly, in the middle of 1940, the war became critical. The arrival of Winston Churchill in 10 Downing Street passed without comment by Wilfrid. On Sunday 26th May the King asked for a National Day of Prayer. *'The war has now taken on a serious aspect'* wrote Wilfrid *'a terrific struggle is taking place in northern France and Belgium. It seems that nearly all the places of worship in Northampton and other parts of the country have been well filled. Mother, Viv and I attend Abington Avenue Chapel and find the attendance to be one of the largest we have ever seen.'*

On 1st June, Wilfrid's 58th birthday, Canadian troops arrived in Northampton. Three of them, Ed, Pat and Craig, were billeted to the Church household. *'Craig and Pat are hot on raw onions'* was one of Wilfrid's few observations. A camp was set up across the road in Abington Park, but it didn't stay long, by June 7th they were moving on. *'The experience was quite an awakening one for all the residents round about here'* wrote Wilfrid. *'Lorry after lorry, gun carriage followed by gun carriage, ambulance, trucks etc. They were only collecting together here preparatory to taking up their quarters further on, probably Aldershot or even to France. The horror of the war is that these and other fine specimens of manhood should risk their lives for what is called freedom by both attacker and defender.'*

It must have brought back memories of the start of the First World War, when thousands of Welsh troops camped on Northampton's Racecourse. *'When such a collection of soldiers, such as these Canadian fellows, meet together in formation and move in long procession through an industrial town as this, we are indeed brought to realise the fact of war.'*

On June 9th, Wilfrid and Naomi walked home from chapel with Bassett-Lowke. He predicted that the Germans would capture Paris and then the war would be over. He was right only about the first part. A week later Wilfrid wrote '*A very momentous day. France asks Germany that she may enter into negotiations. France has been hard pressed, and her armies are now in the most precarious plight. We in this country are wondering how this disaster will affect us. Everyone now realises the greater imminence of attack on our land and it is as if we are awaiting a storm.*' Many of Wilfrid's diary entries at this time have a depressed tone, but he is determined to put on a brave face: '*Personally I am what might be determined stunned and feel considerably overcome by the trend of events. It is very important that I, who hold some small position in life, should set an example of bravery, wisdom and even cheerfulness.*'

Later in June the air raid warnings start. Wilfrid and Naomi had their two grandchildren with them and wake them up to take them to the cellar, the elder one, Christine, is excited by the novelty and thought the experience was good fun.

Philip continued his air force training. On June 24th Wilfrid and Naomi, with Joy, Viv, Florrie and the two granddaughters wait at a pre-arranged time on the edge of Abington Park for their own personal air display. '*We did not have very long to wait as speeding across the park from the north came Phil in his yellow plane (a Miles Magister). He travelled lower and lower and sped over No. 18 at quite a close range and then seemed to disappear over the allotments.*'

On July 2nd, on a trip to Cambridge to visit Naomi's ailing brother-in-law Robert Perry, the road was blocked in places by concrete, old cars, farm implements and old horse carts.

By September, as the bombing of London and major cities started in earnest, a fresh wave of evacuees swept into Northampton. Kent was at risk too. Joy was now living in Tunbridge Wells. Bombs had landed close to her home, so she and her two daughters returned to Northampton, leaving no room for Wilfrid to fulfil his wish to accommodate some more refugees.

On September 11th Wilfrid overheard a woman with her child talking to a group on the pavement near the shop about her experience of the bombs coming down. "*You have no idea*" she said "*what it means to hear those bombs. Bang! Bang! Bang!*" Wilfrid said he felt moved by this 'something welled up, a feeling of horror, disgust and uneasiness. To what depths of degradation can humans sink!!!'

The business was doing well, but it brought Wilfrid little satisfaction. The prospect of the introduction of purchase tax on October 21st was encouraging people to spend. 'Goods representing honest labour are exchanged for pieces of paper representing a guarantee from our government that the printed strip will be kept up to a certain height of power. There seems to be so much uncertainty and instability about and yet we must carry on.'

Vivian had finished at school and the time had come to consider his future. A few months earlier he had expressed an interest in the merchant marine, but that didn't find favour with his father. The idea seemed to have been quietly forgotten. Wilfrid had often noted his younger son's love of an outdoor life, and a career in agriculture seemed to be the answer. They decided to visit Seal Hayne, an agricultural college in Devon. The college were keen to admit Viv, so the principal asked him to start there and then. The seventeen-year-old lad was pleased to be left there while his parents went on to visit Church's China in Paignton before having a short holiday at their seaside second home. Letters home from Viv pleased his father. 'he expresses his growing interest in farming. This is very encouraging as he seems just the type of lad to find pleasure and satisfaction from that great work room under the huge dome of the skies.' He came home for Christmas and spent some time helping in the warehouse. 'At the end of the day he said he preferred farming.'

The novelty of war was fading fast. Despite the air raid warnings, Northampton had still not been attacked. On November 15th Wilfrid, Naomi, Joy and her husband Leslie were in Northampton's Royal Theatre when they heard an air raid warning. Very few people moved, only those who had air raid duties. As the nights close in, so do the blackouts, now running from 5.30pm to 8am. Summertime continued throughout the winter making the mornings particularly dark.

On November 19th an air raid was combined with searchlights criss-crossing the sky. The sound of German planes was heard high above as they passed over the town to more critical targets in the Midlands. From now on that ominous sound could be heard most nights.

Business at the shop continued to be good, but with people wanting to be home before dark, sales were concentrated into a much shorter period. Hire orders from the military stationed around the town were an addition to the usual business. In total, the takings in 1940 showed a sharp increase to £9,142. Wilfrid thought the shop was rather overstocked at the beginning of the year, so the upturn in business had been fortunate for him.

1941- The war at its worst

The war was very quickly to come even closer to home. At 9pm on 15th January 1941 Wilfrid was woken by a loud explosion as the house shook. Three bombs had been unloaded about half a mile away on the Billing Rd. One landing on an out-patients ward of St Andrews Hospital, the only part that was empty of patients at that time. It caused substantial damage and a fire. Another landed in the hospital grounds, and the third in the cemetery across the road. Windows were smashed; fortunately, there were no casualties. The Northampton Mercury reported that a large crater was left in the cemetery, while pieces of gravestones were flung onto nearby roofs. That such attention was paid to the incident demonstrated that Northampton was fortunate not to suffer the mass bombing raids that killed thousands in other towns and cities. At night, the glow of the firestorm engulfing Coventry could be seen from the edge of Northampton.

As stock at the business was being turned into cash, Wilfrid decided to buy another property. 23 St. Davids Rd in Kingsthorpe was the former home of Mr Brown, the town's sanitary inspector. Wilfrid paid £550 for the house and let it at a rent of 13s/6d a week to a couple who had been bombed in Birmingham. '*Am becoming quite a property owner*' he commented. In addition to 18 Abington Park Crescent, he still owned his old homes in Ennerdale Rd, The Avenue Spinney Hill and of course the Devon holiday home, Wyndcroft, which, rather than be left standing empty, he let during the war.

With a young son away in the forces, any loving parents will have in the back of their mind that the next phone call, or a telegram, might bring bad news. Before Christmas, while they were out at a dance, Florrie had taken a call from the RAF in Hastings asking for Mr & Mrs Church, the caller left no message. After a sleepless night and hours of anxiety until the following lunchtime, they had a call from Phil to say that he had been involved in a minor motor accident and had damaged his teeth. Permission from his father was needed for him to have a general anaesthetic for dental work.

On February 1st, 1941 Naomi phoned her husband in a faltering voice. She had received a telegram from Catterick Military Hospital stating that Phil was seriously ill. *'My feelings upon hearing this news were painful'* Wilfrid wrote *'and I expressed myself... 'Good God' and my thoughts took strange fancies such as Phil being subjected to injections etc from modern well-meaning doctors, of Phil nearly 200 miles away lonely.'* Naomi phoned Mr Burrows, so that he should tell Phil's fiancée Eunice. Mr Burrows re-assured him that 'serious' only meant that he was confined to a bed in hospital, if they had said that the illness was 'dangerous', then they should be worried. Poor Florrie *'was very distressed and went moaning and groaning about the house like a fantastic lost soul.'* The next day they drove to Catterick to find a cheerful Philip sitting up in bed rather surprised to see his parents arrive so suddenly. They were told that he would be confined to bed for six weeks. He was better much more quickly than expected and was released in time for him to travel home for his 21st Birthday on 24th February.

On March 2nd Philip told his father that he wished to get married.

'As he was in the RAF and doing precarious duties, he thought it better for him to be married. He spoke as if he only had a fifty-fifty chance of returning from the risky work undertaken

by the RAF. I assured him that is was my opinion that he would eventually return to civil life and that this war might even be over unexpectedly early.

'It was very pathetic to have my son standing there on a bright sunny morn talking of the possibilities of life and death and I naturally felt full of sympathy for him and very troubled in myself.'

Eunice returned from Chapel. *'I met her in the hall, and not telling her of the conversation I had with Phil, gave her a kiss saying, 'this is the first time I have kissed you Eunice'. I think she must have known what I meant for she readily stepped over to me.'*

Phil was told by his medical officer that he was not yet well enough to fly, so he was given another two weeks leave, and the wedding was arranged for 22nd March at Duston Church. Afterwards they took a short honeymoon at Wyndcroft.

On 30th March, Phil returned to his duties at Topcliffe RAF base in Yorkshire. *'I can hardly appreciate the fact that there is a Mrs Philip Church now'*, wrote Wilfrid. *'Another chapter is commencing, and may there be much good to write of during this period.'*

In April a letter arrived from Phil dated

Philip Church married Eunice Burrows at Duston Church.

15th April telling his parents that for the last fortnight he seemed to have lived mostly at night, on duty at the aerodrome. He had his first operational trip over Bordeaux. He is looking forward to Eunice visiting on 21st April.

What happened next is best left for Wilfrid to tell in his own words. He expresses the thoughts and emotions of thousands of parents who find themselves facing the same awful situation in every war.

Saturday April 19th 1941

'Today there has been heavy rain such as will be of great benefit to the crops.

'I was down at business in good time this morning but had not been there long before a phone message came from home and Florrie requested me to come home at once, urgent. As the call was not in M's voice, I wondered what the trouble might be, my mind wandering from M. to Phil, now in his operational flights over enemy territory and to Irene dwelling in London where air raids were being inflicted with great seriousness. My car was parked in Princes St., so I immediately proceeded there and at once made my way home. Here I found Florrie somewhat distressed because of news that had been sent by telegram.

'This was indeed a blow, so I proceed upstairs to find M. who is naturally very disturbed by the message. 'Missing' what pictures that conjures up!

'It was in the back bedroom where we sat and tried to talk, feeling as if we were in a dream. Reality came at intervals and our minds were confused with waves of emotion. We realised we could do nothing except control ourselves and allow the plant of hope to take root within us. The telegram said 'missing' but not missing believed killed and so we await the promised letter hoping that there may be some more encouraging news.

'M full of wisdom and rare sense suggests we carry on with our own work and this we do. M. journeys down to the town to interview the food controller and I enter business again. I don't know how M. faced the crowd and the friends she must have come across, but I do know how difficult it is to appear normal when emotions are surging within. However, I kept the news from my staff until evening time, when I was about to leave for home, I mentioned to Dora what had happened.

'Kind friends have sent M. flowers. Miss Buswell roses, Dora roses, Miss Yorke anemones. These could not have been more pleasing expressions of sympathy.

'During the day I have seen Mr & Mrs Burrows, but I really could not say much and as we met near the Market Place I rather feared to demonstrate my feelings. Mr Burrows suggests, and we all hope, that Phil is a prisoner.

'Eunice would have visited Phil today, she has been at Manchester all the week, and he had arranged for their accommodation at Thirsk. Mr Burrows was in time to send a telegram to Manchester asking her to come back home. Her *uncle brought her back this evening and tomorrow we hope to see Mr & Mrs Burrows and Eunice for tea.'*

Sunday 20th April

'Had rather a restless night with imagination taking me to hopeful and hopeless possibilities. At dawn I look out of the window across the valley and see a clear sky. It seems too early to get up, so I lay hoping to get a little more sleep. This does not come so a few minutes after 6am I get up and dress in garden apparel. Potter about the house for some time making tea, having breakfast and then taking tea up to M. Then to the allotment where I do about an hour's digging. Return home at 10am and as rain descends of the April variety, I paint some parts of the hives. After this I suggest to M. that we have a trip to Castle Ashby. Viv drives the car and the weather having improved we see Castle Ashby under pleasant conditions. On both sides of the Chase were rows of motor mechanised lorries, some hundreds. We walked by the Castle, through the churchyard and into the park where the lakes are. There are signs of spring and the trees were beginning to show life.

'This afternoon about 4pm the Burrows family arrives.... Eunice looked fairly well but rather tired and all of them showed signs of the distressing time being experienced. We too in our own circle show some weariness for this is indeed a trying experience.

'When the conversation turns to Phil, hope is expressed that he will return, that he may be a prisoner in Germany, and so we try to act as if this were actually so. Underneath the terrible uncertainty of it all the anticipation of further news that we hope will be good and the dread of some heavier blow.

'In the evening Mr Burrows and I try to formulate some plan of action. Phil's belongings have to be collected and we shall certainly have to make a journey to Topcliffe.

'It is the letter, promised by the authorities, that we want for now.'

Monday April 21st

'Have received no letter from the R.A.F. in respect of Phil. The waiting is very wearing, and M. woke with a severe headache which caused her to keep in bed all morning. Fortunately, both of us slept quite well last night and this gives us much needed strength. On the way to the shop this morning I gave Mr Reid a lift and he asked me "How the happy couple were going on?" Then the thought crossed my mind-happy!!- I replied with much confusion "I will let you know later on". This reply of course conveyed nothing and Mr Reid was left in the dark as to the news and my feelings.

'During the morning Mr Burrows came in and we consulted about despatching a letter to the C.O. at Topcliffe. This is the communication we sent: -

'Dear Sir,

It is with deep feeling that I am writing to obtain all possible information respecting my son who as advised by telegram on 19th is 'missing'. The 'letter following' has not yet arrived so I am asking if you will kindly let me know all you can, such as the other names of the crew who were on the operational flight with him, also any particular squadron associate of his with whom we might correspond. All information, as you can imagine, will be greatly appreciated.

It is also my intention to visit Topcliffe in a day or two to collect my son's belongings, so I trust therefore that your permission and instruction respecting this will be forthcoming.

So far, we have written to no-one to tell of the distressing experience, but we shall shortly have to send word to our relations whether we obtain further details or not.

Yours sincerely

W.S. Church'

Meanwhile, Eunice had received a letter from RAF Topcliffe. Wilfrid made a copy for his dairy.

No.77 Squadron
Royal Air Force
Topcliffe
Thirsk
Yorks.
19th April 1941
Reference 775/804/1/P3

Dear Mrs Church

It is with deepest sympathy that I write to inform you that your husband, Sergeant P.J. Church was reported missing on the night of 17th April 1941. At the moment there is little information that I can give you, except that he was taking part in an operation sortie over Berlin. I myself was not taking part in the operation that evening, but was in charge of the Operations Room, and from results of my interrogation of pilots taking part, I feel confident that your husband had every chance of making a successful parachute jump, or that the aircraft made a successful landing, and I hope in the near future to receive satisfactory news that he is uninjured and a prisoner of war. Though not being able to guarantee this information I hope to be able to let you have news in the near future.

Your husband joined the squadron in December of last year and proved himself to be an N.C.O. far above the average, and on all operational sorties, he always inspired the other members of the crew with his complete disregard of enemy action, or weather conditions, and by his unfailing devotion to duty. His loss is a severe blow to the squadron, and the whole squadron join me in this expression of sympathy with you in your time of anxiety.

Yours sincerely
Jarman
Wing Commander, commanding No 77 Squadron. RAF

On 25th April Wilfrid and Naomi, with Mr & Mrs Burrows, Viv and Eunice set off for RAF Topcliffe, near Thirsk in Yorkshire.

'In a little office about 10ft x 10ft square leading off the hangar we find Flt. Lieut. Brown seated at his desk busy at the phone and interviewing various supernumeraries. The office is furnished with steel boxes, maps, photo's etc and the doors are painted green. We are unable to get any further particulars of Phil's whereabouts. We are told that two of the planes that ventured from this 'drome are missing and that one contained the crew of which Phil was a member. It is presumed that during the attack on Berlin nine of our bombers were reported missing, one crew was picked up in the sea by a speed boat, after only half an hour's immersion (this crew was definitely not the one we were seeking), another crew made a forced landing in Holland and this crew might have been the one we are concerned about. The officer thought there was a very good chance of Phil being a prisoner. This therefore is about all the information we were able to obtain from Flt. Lieut. Brown.'

The family party also met Sidney Munns, an old school friend of Phil's who was flying on the same air raid. Wing Commander Munns wrote the following many years later in his memoirs 'As luck would have it', published in 1992.

'We carried out the attack at 0100 hours in very heavy flak, and just after I had released the bombs we could clearly see an explosion ahead of us and a Whitley going down in flames. Sadly I was later to discover that it was my old school chum Phil Church and his crew going down. His was the only aircraft missing that night. …

'Next morning the CO asked me to take part in a "committee of adjustment"- to collect Phil Church's belongings from his room etc., and a few days later I met his young widow, Eunice, when she came to collect them. It was a very sad duty to perform.'

Whatever Sidney Munns said to Eunice, her hope, and that of her in-laws, was that her new husband was still alive.

The group spent the night in the 'Golden Fleece' Hotel in Thirsk, where Eunice had already been booked to stay by Phil. During dinner they met Sergeant Wheatley, who shared quarters with Phil, and he too reassured them that he might be a prisoner. Learning of Viv's interest in agriculture he says he would prefer to be working a farm tractor at two miles an hour than piloting a plane at 200 miles an hour. *'We felt that these young fellows were not relishing the devastating work they were ordered to undertake'* wrote Wilfrid *'The term 'madness' is far away too mild an expression to use.'*

The next day they returned to Northampton, Viv driving Phil's car with Eunice. All they could do was wait for further news. Letters of hope and sympathy poured in from friends and relations. Wilfrid wrote to the next of kin of the other three members of Phil's crew asking them to share any knowledge that they receive.

On May 5th Mr Barrows of Balmoral Rd called at the shop to say that his son had been reported missing. He had been out on the same night as Phil, but not in the same squadron. In the evening Naomi visited Mr and Mrs Barrows, who had just received news that their son was a prisoner of war. *'I felt keyed up to receive such a message'* wrote Wilfrid.

He was now spending several nights sharing fire watch duty in the Emporium Arcade. Some of Wilfrid's fellow firewatchers placed their camp beds in an empty shop, but he had his in his office. Constantly anxious for Phil, he slept badly, and spent the day at work, tired.

A talk by Margaret Bondfield at the Town Hall on 9th May spurred him on in his voluntary work. Northampton's former MP was speaking on behalf of the Ministry of Information. *'Miss M.B. is looking decidedly older, and as the light was shed on her features, she appeared rather an old woman.'* It was 37 years since a young Margaret Bondfield shared the stage with Wilfrid's father in support of the implementation of the shop hours act.

On 11th May, news comes in of one of the worst bombing raids on London. The Houses of Parliament were damaged, 1,400 people were killed. Wilfrid noted that 33 German bombers were brought down, and British aircraft attacked Hamburg and other German cities. Wilfrid and Naomi now had to await news of Irene. Was she safe in London? There was no news and now they had two of their children to worry about.

With thoughts returning to Phil, Wilfrid wrote. *'It is strange what thoughts come rising up in the mind at this time. Have I been fair to my own son? Have I given him that instruction and advice that a father should? Have I been too reticent with him when I might have shown some demonstration of affection?*

'M waits patiently and bravely but when she at first heard the news that Phil was missing, she said 'There seemed to be something break within me'. Eunice appears bright and has strong hopes of Phil's return.'

On 13th May, another letter arrived to bring a glimmer of hope. Mrs Boon, the wife of one of Phil's crew members wrote: 'I have received news from the Red Cross Society that my husband has been killed. … If you have not had any news, I should think it is a hopeful sign that your son is safe.'

The next day they learned that Irene was safe. They had failed contact by phone, but Irene sent a letter describing the blitz as the worst she had experienced.

On May 16th, Naomi's sister Rachel, and her husband Ernest arrive from Cambridge for a visit. The four of them attended a matinee performance of 'Major Barbara' by Bernard Shaw. Wilfrid described what awaited them on their return to Abington Park Crescent.

'Upon the return home Ern and I stroll down the garden and there near the low wall dividing the lower garden from the wilderness stand M. and Rach. They appeared to be looking towards the rock garden but as I approach closer I notice that M. is weeping … she tells me that a letter has indeed arrived and that it is on the mantelshelf behind my photograph.

'My feelings cannot be completely described, and I feel unable to think or concentrate. M came with me by the fire and there we felt the bitterness of the blow. Ern and Rach moved into the kitchen where Florrie was and they were able to give Florrie some needed comfort,

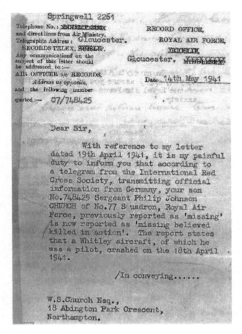
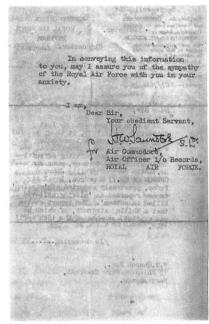

Springwell 2261

Telephone No.: XXXXXXXXXX
and direct lines from Air Ministry.
Telegraphic Address: Gloucester.
RECORDS TELEX, XXXXX.
Any communications on the
subject of this letter should
be addressed to:—
AIR OFFICER i/c RECORDS,
Address as opposite,
and the following number
quoted:— 07/748425

RECORD OFFICE,
ROYAL AIR FORCE,
XXXXXX
Gloucester. XXXXXXX

Date 14th May 1941

Dear Sir,

With reference to my letter
dated 19th April 1941, it is my painful
duty to inform you that according to
a telegram from the International Red
Cross Society, transmitting official
information from Germany, your son
No.748425 Sergeant Philip Johnson
CHURCH of No.77 Squadron, Royal Air
Force, previously reported as 'missing'
is now reported as 'missing believed
killed in action'. The report states
that a Whitley aircraft, of which he
was a pilot, crashed on the 18th April
1941.

/In conveying......

W.S.Church Esq.,
18 Abington Park Crescent,
Northampton.

In conveying this information
to you, may I assure you of the sympathy
of the Royal Air Force with you in your
anxiety.

I am,
Dear Sir,
Your obedient Servant,

Air Commodore,
Air Officer i/c Records,
ROYAL   AIR   FORCE.

because poor girl she loved Phil with an affection as great as possible. Phil was to her a part of her life and will always retain that position. …

'M and I being left alone in the living room together feel how important it now is that we shall do something useful in life, whatever that may be, but grief overwhelms us and as I write this all seems a dream.'

'Did I understand Phil? He seemed to live in half a dream, it seemed he was almost pre-destined for something, he had no desire to take up any particular calling, he was kind, lacked viciousness and could harm no-one, and yet this hellish war fever and military machine dragged this gentle soul to do that which he abhorred.'

Wilfrid's diary continued with memories. Of Phil as a twelve-year-old boy playing rugby. Of a glimpse caught of him leaning over the garden gate with a pipe in his mouth, and of his first day working in the shop.

'Ern and Rach return [to Cambridge] *about 9pm, taking us to Little Houghton from whence we walk across the fields back home, talking, talking, talking, rather sorrowfully on the way.'*

The next day, Wilfrid had to tell Eunice. *'It was very painful duty on my part and I almost broke down during the ordeal. I was expecting that Eunice had also received a similar notification, but this has not happened. Seeing how moved I was at the disclosure Eunice threw her arms around my neck and said words to some such effect as 'Oh no, it cannot be, I am sure he will come back, why do they write such letters?'* Her reaction surprised Wilfrid, and he felt glad that she had not lost hope.

The Northampton branch of the British Legion had been making enquiries about missing Northampton service men. They informed Wilfrid on 21st May that German sources had informed the British Red Cross in Geneva that all the crew of Phil's plane had lost their lives. *'This letter gives us no hope'* concludes Wilfrid.

Nearly six months later. on November 14th, Wilfrid and Naomi received a card from Buckingham Palace. Later the same day an official letter from the Records Office of the RAF confirmed Phil's death. He was buried in September 1942 at the Charlottenburg war cemetery in Berlin. At his parents and his widow's request, there was no special message on his gravestone. Two years after the war, his grave was moved to the British Military Cemetery in Berlin.

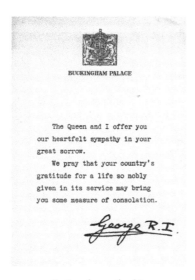

Letter from the king.   *Phil Church in flying gear.*

Town centre crash

On the night of 14th July, Wilfrid was on fire watch duty in the arcade with three others. They played cards until after midnight, he went back to his office, assembled his camp bed and after reading for a few minutes took off his shoes and coat and climbed into bed. As usual he didn't sleep well, waking several times.

'About 4.45am I was awakened by a tremendous roaring sound just overhead. Jumping up and pulling aside the 'blackout' I looked across the Market Square and saw clouds of smoke rolling up by All Saints Church. Flames lighted up these clouds with a ruddy glow and the continuous explosion of cartridge was heard. A Stirling four engine bomber had crashed right in the centre of the town, crumbling up and burning fiercely in the space at the top of Bridge St. and for a few yards down Gold St.

'As quickly as possible I jumped up, put on my shoes, raced down the stairs to the arcade entrance, where I found the other three members of the Arcade Fire Watch Association who were on duty with me last night. We ran across the Market Square, through Drum Lane and the spectacle of burning debris presented itself. Splintering glass was falling on the pavements, wardens were moving quickly about endeavouring to cut off the flames.

'The south west end of All Saints Church was caught in the flames and smoke was issuing from the windows. Palmers, the Tailors, at the top end of Bridge St had flames leaping up inside their second floor and soon their plate glass in all their windows came crashing out. Bells, the ironmongers, Burtons at the bottom of College St and the Queens Head adjoining were all severely damaged. It did not seem wise to venture too near the conflagration as bombs might have been about yet unexploded.

'Then came the fire engines and unrolling hose pipes from many hydrants the flames were soon being subjugated by streams of water. All this was a wondrous sight and of course I could

Scenes After The Plane Crash In Northampton

Great Fire-Fighting And Relief Work By Volunteers

PROMPT AND GALLANT ACTION on the part of Northampton's regular and volunteer fire brigades, police, A.R.P. services, and demolition squads averted any extension of the damage caused by the plane which crashed in the centre of the town, with effects pictured on this page and page 1.

From the Northampton Independent 1941.

not but think of the occupants of the aeroplane, were they safe? My imagination showed me Phil being hurled down from some terrible height and meeting his fate thus.

'The place crashed at dawn, and the duskiness gave colour to the burning but soon the morning light came attended by rain.'

Wilfrid cycled home, where he found that one of the crew had safely landed by parachute in Abington Park. The pilot was killed when his parachute failed to open, his body was found on Kingsthorpe Recreation Ground. The only civilian casualty was a cyclist who broke his leg. Part of the engine of the plane was found on the roof of the church. The RAF Stirling Bomber had apparently been damaged by flak, and on the way home had run out of fuel.

For Wilfrid this incident was the worst he would personally encounter during the war. Travelling, he saw the severe bomb damage in London, Birmingham and elsewhere. His daughter Irene lived through the blitz in London and Joy and her family suffered the damage caused by 'doodlebugs' in Kent in the final months of the war. The fear carried on, but there was no more trauma for the Church family on the level they experienced from April to July 1941. From now on, it was about rationing, austerity, and as the war turned the corner in 1943, it was about preparing for its end and what was to come afterwards.

Church's China during the war

However bad things are, if there is food of some kind to eat, people need plates and bowls. That means business of some kind for Church's China. As the war progressed, Church's stock of decorative items without function declined. There were no imported goods and the manufacture of luxury goods was restricted by the government. The famous Stoke on Trent manufacturers were permitted only to produce utility items. That meant not just cups, saucers, plates and bowls but pudding basins, pie dishes and mixing bowls. Despite the difficulty in sourcing products to sell, the takings at Church's China continued to grow. Rising from £6,490 in 1939 to £15,643 in 1945.

Church's China had a large hire business. There was demand from the local military, as well as catering china for hospitals and other institutions. In October 1941 over 3,000 plates were delivered from Stoke manufacturer Susie Cooper Ltd. By December, gaps were appearing on the shelves and with the difficulty in buying stock, capital was being turned into cash, so Wilfrid began buying shares.

His relationship with his suppliers meant Wilfrid could buy more stock than some other retailers. In 1942, for the first time, the shop opened on Good Friday. '...so many goods had arrived for unpacking, and we were so in arrears as far as work was concerned that we kept open until 5pm.'

The following day there were record takings- £156. 'Money flows in too freely, this probably on account of a shortage and also because customers have arrived from Coventry and Rugby where we are told there is difficulty in obtaining goods.' On April 10th he took the car out (use was restricted due to petrol rationing) to deliver orders to village schools in Walgrave, Broughton and Gretton.

Wilfrid had to manage his limited stock carefully. *'Customers are keen to buy, and I have to refuse to sell to many of them.'* On 2nd May he wrote *'Today has had almost a Christmas volume of business except that instead of a great demand for goods as seasonal gifts there have been many customers hoping to obtain goods before the decorated and luxurious class are prohibited.'*

As stocks dwindled, he called on Naomi's skills to assemble oddments to make up saleable sets. *'Every day seems full and I am very occupied, perhaps not in such a selfish manner as I should be, but nevertheless I feel business needs very careful thought and understanding. We are often puzzled whether to sell what we have on hand or reserve some stock so that sales can be distributed more evenly year by year.'*

Other people would have been happy to be taking money, but not Wilfrid. In July 1942 he wrote *'Business is still of rather unsatisfactory character. The demand is greater than the supply. Plenty of money is in evidence as was shown today when Mrs Barratt bought two dinner sets- one for £40 and another for £17 17s. As it happens, I am not requiring the cash and may find some difficulty in finding a resting place for it. My stock is fairly good, but I am by no means anxious to sell as I feel that my pieces of china and glass are more useful than the scraps of paper tendered in payment.'*

A high turnover of cheap, bulky products means more work in the warehouse. Joe Gunn, Church's warehouseman had been working in the shop since the early 1920's. He was called up to the army and left on 25th July 1942, leaving Wilfrid on his own to struggle with enormous crates of tableware. He re-organised his work, getting help from other staff and family when available. Joe was a rather reluctant conscript, but for some unexplained reason he was not gone long, returning after a year.

Wilfrid made an estimate of the volume of goods he sold in 1942, mostly plain white or cream crockery. The list included 1,728 dozen earthenware cups and saucers.

In October 1943 Wilfrid and Naomi spent two days in Stoke on Trent trying to buy more stock. At the Copeland showroom he was promised a few dozen decorative items produced by special licence. The next day they were shown around Wedgwood's brand-new factory just outside the city at Barlaston. Utility pieces were being turned out for the home market, anything fancy was only being made in small quantities, and mostly for the American market. The only success in buying anything decorated was at the Minton factory, where they were offered a 26-piece dessert set for £76, which Wilfrid thought was rather expensive. In today's money (2019) this would be about £3,400, but he bought it anyway and considered splitting it up. In fact, he never sold it, and pieces remain with various members of the family.

Business continued in much the same way for the rest of the war. Wilfrid was astonished to be taking over £100 a day in the lead up to Christmas 1944, but finished up with very little left to sell. With just four days left to Christmas, he closed the shop for the day just to sort and price what little he had left. On the final Saturday before Christmas the shop took over £250, a new record.

By early 1945 two showrooms of the shop were completely empty, so Joe Gunn was put to work whitewashing the walls.

Joy, Irene and Eunice

After the loss of Phil, Wilfrid and Naomi's worries about their remaining children continued for the rest of the war. Joy, Leslie and their two daughters were now living in Tunbridge Wells in Kent. They were not free from bombing raids until the final year of the war. The threat was from what Wilfrid called pilotless planes. Doodlebugs, V-1 and V-2 rockets that could strike London and Kent from the north coast of France and Belgium. Joy reported that the anti-aircraft firing caused a great deal of distress in the town, she found a piece of shrapnel in the roof of her house. Wilfrid and Naomi took care of the children for long periods, and sometimes Joy joined them in Northampton. In October 1942 Joy and Leslie's third child, Stuart, was born.

Irene had witnessed some of the worst of the bombing in both Birmingham and London. In the summer of 1940 she met Henry Soper, a research chemist studying for his PhD. They married in February 1942. Wilfrid often complained that Henry spent too much time engrossed in his books to pay Irene much attention. Their first child, Phyllida, was born just after the end of the war.

Eunice, widowed by Phil's death only a month after their marriage, continued to visit her parents in law regularly. Her family shared Christmas day 1941 at Abington Park Crescent and they visited again to share the first anniversary of the wedding. Wilfrid settled his son's estate with Mr Burrows, making Eunice the main beneficiary.

In July 1943 Eunice married again. Her new husband was Stanley Page, who went on to start an oil recycling business, Duston Oils, which is still run by his family today. Wilfrid and Naomi were invited to the wedding, but they declined, feeling the strain would have been too much for them.

Vivian

In April 1941 Viv took four examinations at the Royal Agricultural Society in Leeds for a National Diploma in Agriculture. Due to illness, he passed just two of the four of them and he returned to Seal Hayne after his brother's death.

For a time, Viv's work and training exempted him from call-up. On a visit to Seal Hayne in June 1941 Wilfrid wrote '*We were glad to see how well Vivian was looking and how cheerful he appeared to be in his agricultural work. We feel somewhat concerned about his future attitude towards army enlistment and we should be relieved to know that he was so interested in his agricultural work that he found satisfaction in doing it without much thought of what others might think he ought to do. ... 'the pull of militarism has its power'.*

In April 1942 Viv wrote home to say that he had applied to defer his National Service to enable him to complete his diploma course. He had joined the Home Guard in Newton Abbott, but even the small

Devonshire town had not escaped a bombing raid. *'I was on guard on Friday and we had a bomb burst only 100 yards away from the Drill Hall'* he told his parents *'It bust all our windows and killed four fire watchers nearby. It was rather terrifying.'* On a trip to Seal Hayne the next month, the farm manager told Wilfrid that his son is 'the best of his students and a 'cert' for the diploma. In August Viv told his father that he wanted to be a pilot in the RAF before the war was over. Wilfrid commented *'A lad of his size must feel self-conscious in the midst of so many in uniforms, and when the question is asked of him 'what are you when not in civvies?' it is indeed an embarrassing moment. Twice in my presence has Viv been faced with some such query.'*

Wilfrid became increasingly concerned that his son's work in the Home Guard and his wish to join the RAF were getting in way of his agricultural studies. On Naomi's birthday, 31st March 1943, a letter arrived from Viv to say that he believed he was almost certain to fail his college exams. Wilfrid records this depressing news in his diary, but at bottom of the page he adds *'since writing the above page Vivian phoned through to say that he has passed his college exam.'* However, he needed to go back to Leeds for his National Diploma exam, but once again, was taken ill at exam time, jaundice preventing him from making the journey.

Wilfrid asked the principal of Seal Hayne if his son could get a further deferment of his National Service to enable him to take his second-year course again, but it seems the only option was for Viv to seek special leave from the forces to get a week's revision before taking the exam again next April.

Fortunately, Viv's jaundice was not too severe, and on the 19th June 1943, he passed his medical to join the RAF with a view to joining the crew of a bomber. Wilfrid didn't share Viv's excitement at this news. *'I was rather affected by the report he came home with, but I can see that this is what he had hoped to be, and any other result would certainly have disappointed. ... To one with pacifist ideas the launching forth of a son into the field of battle is indeed a confusion of thought and a shaking of convictions.'*

Vivian Church in uniform.

Viv was told to report for duty at the Lords Cricket Ground on 27th June. Soon after, he was transferred to Scarborough for training, where he was billeted in the Grand Hotel.

Early in 1944 it became clear that Viv would be stationed abroad to complete his training. Letters home were strictly censored as it was clearly important that the enemy should not know that a ship with thousands of future air crews was on the open seas.

Father and son hatched a little plot. They agreed that if he is sent abroad, his letter will indicate the destination by the first letter of a postscript. A for Africa, C for Canada and I for India.

On 14th January Viv wrote from Manchester that this would be his last letter for some time. *'The weather has been deadly lately, snow, rain, ice and fog all combined with a beautiful grey black Manchester slush. Afraid I cannot say any more.'*

P.S. Arthur sends his kindest regards.'

So, Wilfrid knew that his son was bound for Africa, but where in Africa? Another letter didn't arrive until 9th March. *'Censorship is exceptionally strong'* wrote Viv *'so I can't give you any idea where I am at the moment. Life is really rather dull; we sleep in hammocks which is rather strange and dangerous at first but I have mastered the art of getting in and only come out now when I really mean to …. I have just learnt that I am allowed to say that I am at sea.'*

Without much to do, there was plenty of time for discussions on board ship. *'This morning we had a most interesting discussion on the pro's and cons of communism and state ownership. The discussion started when one lucky lad produced 6 ships biscuits. Naturally he was all against communal ownership whereas we were all for it. We were in the majority and extracted the biscuits from the bloated capitalist.'* One of the other men on the ship was Tony Benn.

The attraction of the adventure was wearing thin. *'I feel rather homesick at the moment and wish the whole thing was over and we could all go to Wyndcroft for long drives in the car together'*, he wrote.

The long sea voyage through the Mediterranean, the Suez canal, the Red Sea and down the coast of East Africa took about three months. Wilfrid was delighted on March 16th to receive a letter from Viv that he had arrived in South Africa and was stationed near Durban.

Viv's letters home gave a colourful picture of South Africa. He wrote enthusiastically about the landscape, the sea and the mountains and the people. Luxuries were still to be found, and he sent home parcels of crystallised fruit and chocolate. Wilfrid and Naomi enjoyed these letters, and some of them were transcribed in their entirety into the diary. Viv looked forward to his parents visiting South Africa one day, and he sent tourist brochures home. He did not write about the inequality and racism he encountered, but his experiences there made him a lifelong opponent of apartheid.

On 20th February 1945 Wilfrid and Naomi learned that Viv had been promoted. *'We do hope that his stay in S. Africa may continue longer, especially as we rather fear that any move to such a place as England may take him to more uninteresting quarters and cause him ultimate dis-satisfaction.'* It was not to be. A little over a month later the phone rang, Viv was in Harrogate, having boarded a fast transport ship home.

He was back in Northampton for his mother's 62nd Birthday on 31st March 1945.

'I was performing what is called 'toilet' at the time when Irene opens the door of the bathroom to inform me that Vivian had arrived...'

'Having hurriedly fixed my teeth in position I venture forth to meet my son, who has been absent from home about sixteen

months, nearly all of this time being a training period in South Africa. Vivian was in the hall and we enthusiastically met … It was the same Viv with his deep voice… He is very pleased to be home again, and we listen to his many experiences and his varied accounts of his travel, doings, associations and to his opinion about natives and their mannerisms.'

Viv was home for two weeks leave, the war may be almost over, but his service in the RAF was not yet finished.

Preparing for D Day

The Church family's holiday home in Devon was to play its part in bringing the war to an end.

Early in the war, using Wyndcroft for holidays became a practical impossibility. Petrol rationing made getting there difficult, and the demands of business and family gave them little time for long holidays. The military interest in this area was also apparent at an early stage. On a visit in 1940, Wilfrid noted that empty houses had been requisitioned. On a walk through the nearby village of Strete to a favourite spot he called 'Happy Valley' he saw 'dug outs, trenches and barbed wire entanglements'. He avoided going close to the sea due to landmines. Soldiers were in Matts Point House (formerly Penlee), below Wyndcroft.

In 1941 the house was let to an elderly couple who made it their home for two years, but at the end of November 1943 Wilfrid received notice from the Admiralty that the Wyndcroft was to be requisitioned. The tenants had to leave in a hurry, the house had to be cleared of as much furniture and belongings as possible. An article in the Times reported that 3,000 people were to be evacuated in an area of 45 to 50 square miles of the South Devon coast. It was to be used as a training ground for the US Army. Protests from local farmers were to no avail, they had to be gone by Christmas.

Wilfrid and Naomi stayed in Dartmouth while arranging the removal of furniture to Paignton. The 1st of December was a 'delightful day' so they decided to walk to Wyndcroft. Coming down the hill into the Blackpool Valley they found the road was blocked to all traffic by an overturned American tank. Blackpool beach was being used for landing practices. *This district is being taken over by American forces and it is presumed that some very realistic manoeuvres will be undertaken when live ammunition will be in evidence,'* wrote Wilfrid. The evacuation of the area for US military exercises was public knowledge reported in national newspapers. It may have been a reasonable assumption by Wilfrid that it would be used to prepare for D Day. He continued *'These actions bring many casualties. It is considered probable that from this district the invasion may be launched or that it may be one of the invasion points.'* His prediction about casualties was absolutely, right. Uncannily so.

The full facts weren't revealed until long after Wilfrid's death. In April 1944, The American commanders ordered that live ammunition should be used in an exercise at Slapton Sands. Only this way, they thought, would the troops get the real sense of working under enemy fire while landing on the beaches. Due to friendly fire, and an attack by German U boats operating out of Cherbourg, 749 American soldiers and sailors lost their lives. The death toll was made worse by poor communications and poor training. Many soldiers drowned at sea or died of hypothermia, simply because they had not been shown how to wear a life belt correctly. It was the worst loss of life in a training exercise in the war, remaining largely unknown until the 1980s, when the research of a Devon man, Ken Small, shone a spotlight on the disaster in his book 'The Forgotten Dead'.

In January 1945, Wyndcroft was released from requisition. Wilfrid visited in March, finding that the house was in good condition. It is well away from the sea, and a couple of miles from the main focus of the exercise at Slapton Sands. He visited Torcross, the village at the other end of the long beach, where damage was already being repaired by Italian prisoners, and people were returning to their homes. He saw that The Royal Sands Hotel had been reduced to a pile of rubble. It is now the site of a car park and a memorial to the fateful exercise.

The Chiparus statue

Holidays during the war were mostly reduced to a few days snatched while visiting one of the children. Wyndcroft could not be used but Wilfrid and Naomi did take holidays in Wales and the Lake District.

In May 1944 Wilfrid and Naomi spent a fortnight at Derwent Water in the Lake District with the Holiday Fellowship. As with most Lake District holidays it was cold and wet, patches of snow were still visible on the mountain tops, but they still ventured out for long guided walks. On the way home, they stopped at Bowness, where a gift shop was selling goods in aid of the YWCA overseas. *'we entered the shop and made a few purchases'* wrote Wilfrid, *'one being a figure on a plinth for which I paid £10/10s. M. did not care for it but my taste was towards it and so we had it carefully packed up and wondered however we should be able to carry all our belongings home.'*

'Footsteps' by Demetre Chiparus.

Did Wilfrid really know what he had bought? The art deco sculpture of a dancing lady in ivory and bronze stood on a polished marble plinth. It was by one of most celebrated art deco sculptors, Demetre Chiparus.

£10/10s in 1944 is equivalent to about £450 in 2019. Today, Chiparus sculptures of this quality are worth over £20,000. He did carry it home successfully and it stood in pride of place in their living room. Naomi used to say that it was bought in memory of Phil.

The end of the war

On the 18th January 1943, a speaker at Rotary lunch gave a talk on the recently published Beveridge Report. The Liberal academic Sir William Beveridge was commissioned by the wartime coalition to report on the future social insurance. It identified five great obstacles to post war reconstruction, Want, Disease, Ignorance, Squalor and Idleness. It set out the framework for the development of the post war welfare state.

Wilfrid was impressed. *'This insurance scheme promises to be of outstanding merit, and I have bought a copy-a full one- and I hope to delve into its suggestions and plannings sometime. This will be an excellent mental exercise.'* Two weeks later he found it hard going *'There are about three hundred pages in this book and as it contains many figures, extracts and legal expressions it will be a lengthy study. Am afraid such reading is very difficult for me. It does appear to contain many wise suggestions and plans for the post war effort and should it but partly succeed will indeed have been worthwhile.'*

During 1943 and 1944 Wilfrid often reported the sound of bombers roaring overhead, on their way to raids over Germany. There were still many evacuees in Northampton. The Rotary club organised entertainments and events for them, and he was a key organiser.

Wilfrid rarely writes about the progress of the war. D Day passes without comment, but by September 1944 it was becoming clear to him that the end was in sight. *'...some sections of the allied army are within the borders of Germany'* he wrote. *'There is the prospect of an early termination of hostilities and many in high authority speak very enthusiastically of the likelihood of German collapse and the hope of Japan being overwhelmed. Next week the 'black-out' will cease and it will indeed be a relief to have brighter lighting in the streets and less blackness and stuffiness in the homes.'* His prediction a few days later that Germany would capitulate at any time was premature, no doubt due to some wishful thinking.

Around this time Wilfrid's writing is often quite depressive, despite the prospect of the end of the war. The weather and the changing of the seasons were a major subject of the diaries, maybe they affected his mood. He wrote this on 1st October 1944.

'The days are perceptibly becoming shorter and today has been dreary and even rather depressing. It is difficult to know how to find enjoyment and satisfaction now-a-days. I suppose the background of the war has much to do with these feelings and yet I feel my spirits should be more pleasant than they are.'

He often expressed a feeling of guilt for his lifestyle *'There are those who would tell me to live a more unselfish life and no doubt such an existence would give a zest to happiness.'* He goes on to report the German surrender of Calais, and Montgomery's prediction that the war would be over by Christmas, while Churchill predicted that victory would come sometime in 1945.

As the troops advanced, news of the suffering of the civilian population on the continent came home. On 16th October a speaker from the Society of Friends gave a moving account to Rotary on the conditions in Europe. *'his report on the terrible sufferings of the populations especially the children and old people was very moving.'* At the Friends Meeting House on 26th November Wilfrid and Naomi found themselves in agreement with a speaker, who had lived in Germany, stressing the importance of friendship with Germany. He commented *'it may be that proportionally there are as many bad English as bad Germans'.*

There was another step towards the end of the war on 3rd December. Wilfrid spent some time at the shop on a Sunday to enable a cable to be fitted for a loudspeaker in the Market Square. The Northampton Home Guard were being disbanded with a final parade.

Northampton Council were planning for life after the war. Councillor Lee spoke to the Rotary club in January 1945 on the future of Northampton. *'This address was of outstanding interest as he dealt with the planning of the town...'* wrote Wilfrid. *'The new roads and widened thoroughfares appeared on a large plan behind the speaker and those particularly who knew Northampton were able to follow with fascination the course of his explanations. I felt how important it was that such planning should be undertaken at an early date. Councillor Lee enthuses on his subject and is certainly the right person to deal with the matter.'*

The report in the Northampton Mercury gave more detail. Councillor Frank Lee divided the town into four quarters centred on All Saints Church. The south west quarter was to be zoned for warehousing and light industrial uses, containing the gas works and the railway station. The south east quarter containing Becketts Park was zoned for open space, the north west for residential and the north east as the civic centre of the town. Councillor Lee called for new industries to be drawn to the town to replace the declining boot and shoe industry. He predicted that technical improvements in shoe making would mean that in 30 to 50 years the number of operatives would be reduced by half.

Wilfrid wrote nothing more on the progress of the war until 1st May 1945, when he reported the the news of Hitler's death. *'Last week Mussolini was killed and now this great upheaval which has distressed so many for the last six years is rapidly assuming a very different complexion. The fall of Berlin is expected and the greatest of all reports is surely near at hand and that is the unconditional surrender of Germany.'*

There were still moments of pain. Wilfrid reported that a man leaving the shop said: 'We shall soon have the lads home again'. *'I replied that one of my sons would not return. He glanced at me and made no reply.'*

Wilfrid was thinking about how he will feel when the war is declared to be over.

'When the cessation of hostilities is declared M. and I do not feel like rejoicing, but arrangements are already being drawn up for two-day celebrations. We have a strange feeling about the present events, pangs of disillusionment, a lack of faith in human nature and a revelation of many horrors that we had not thought of.' The next day came news of

the German surrender in Italy and the fall of Berlin, but the news of total surrender had still not come through.

At Chapel in 6th May the preacher in one of his prayers mentioned conscientious objectors. *'I rather wondered how the congregation would react to this'* wrote Wilfrid. In the evening they learn that Winston Churchill will broadcast to the nation on May 10th and the 'V Day' with be prior to that. Wilfrid's thoughts turned to the future. *'I suppose political problems will loom rather large. Then too the desire of the forces for demobilisation. Arrangements by the allies for an army of occupation. All these tremendous events will require understanding, tact and endless work.'* The next day he noted that the unconditional surrender documents had been signed.

Finally, on May 8th, V.E. Day arrived. Wilfrid reported that many people had gone to London for the celebrations and the town was rather quiet. He and Naomi were planning to go to the town centre in the evening, but the wireless persuaded them to stay at home. *'This broadcast was one of the most marvellous we have ever heard,'* wrote Wilfrid. *'it was arranged with efficiency and with such telling sequence. Accounts of the London celebrations came through with the accompanying broadcasts of sounds, such as the cheers and noises from the crowds. Colonial and foreign broadcasts were interspersed with telling effect. In spite of all of this there was the thought behind those who would never return, those who had lost their lives, the flower of the land. Also, the cloud in the east where Japanese aggression is so distressing was much in our thought.*

'To get the European war over is a great event, the greatest historic happening of our times.'

CHAPTER SEVEN

AUSTERITY TO PROSPERITY

THE WAR WAS OVER, AND WITH IT HAD GONE THE BLACKOUTS, the air raid warnings and most importantly Wilfrid's fear for his family. In most other ways though, life carried on much as before. Rationing and austerity continued. Church's China could still only obtain undecorated utility goods for sale. Vivian was still serving in the RAF, not flying aircraft, but learning to drive heavy goods vehicles and tractors, and to operate road drills and cement mixers.

Wilfrid went to hear Clement Attlee speak at Northampton Town Hall during the 1945 General Election. He was persuaded to vote Labour, which he continued to do in subsequent general elections. Naomi liked the Liberal candidate, and Wilfrid thought she voted accordingly.

Resistance to Refugees

News gradually emerged of the atrocities carried out by the Nazis. In July 1945, Wilfrid bought 20 Abington Park Crescent, just two doors away from his home. It is a large detached house, originally built to be at one end of a terrace of fine Edwardian houses overlooking Abington Park, but the rest were never built. Wilfrid's intention was to turn it into two flats, and that is what he eventually did. However, news was emerging of the atrocities carried out by the Nazis, and in October he accepted a request to temporarily let the house as a home to Jewish refugee boys from Germany. This did not please a neighbour, on 22nd October he received a letter from a solicitor objecting to the house being used for refugees.

> 'Our client has asked us to say that... he thinks it is most unfortunate that at a time when our fighting men, returning home, are having the greatest difficulty in finding houses, property should be let to foreigners, who even though they may be deserving of sympathy, have far less claim for consideration than our own fighting men.'

Wilfrid was annoyed by this unsympathetic letter, but he didn't rise to the bait:- *'taking many things into consideration, for one the necessity of remaining on good terms with neighbours, I replied rather briefly as follows: 'replying to yours of Oct. 22nd the property mentioned has been let for six months, the termination of the period to be in April 1946.'*

An article in the Chronicle and Echo on December 14th reported that 15 Jewish boys from Poland were arriving to stay at a hostel, run by Professor Isidore Marks on behalf of the Jewish Refugees Committee. All the boys were either orphans or their parents could not be traced, but their physical or psychological condition was such that they could not stay with families.

The tenancy overran. At the beginning of May 1946, another solicitor's letter arrived. This time Wilfrid appealed for a little compassion.

> *'The tenancy expired in April and I was quite under the impression that the tenant would then be leaving',* he replied to the solicitor. *'He has however been unable to find other accommodation. The youths who are under Dr Marks have been rescued from concentration camps, some having been branded*

by the Nazis, and I believe, none able to tell whether their parents are living or not.

'The boys are being carefully looked after and hope to be absorbed into industry, or, as they ardently hope, be sent to Palestine. I feel sure that [the neighbour] *will show a sympathetic appreciation to the position.'*

The solicitor replied: *'With regard to your final paragraph whilst one's natural instincts are to sympathise with homeless refugees, we must point out that it is easier to sympathise from a safe and convenient distance than from actually next door.*

'Abington Park Crescent is essentially a high-class residential area and one cannot imagine a more unsuitable place to install a hostel for foreign Jewish refugees. The result as far as my client is concerned is that what was once a quiet and peaceful spot has been turned into a sort of bedlam....'

Wilfrid was only one door further away from the refugee boys than the complainant, who had a high brick wall separating his garden from No.20. He forwarded the letter to Dr Marks and pressed him to find alternative accommodation. Dr Marks replied *'...it is impossible to accommodate these boys in private families- they have suffered in their tender childhood so immensely that they need an immense patience in their education to give them back their belief in human kindness- thus their excitement and somewhat loud voices.'* Dr Marks concluded that the letter was *'dictated obviously by antisemitics, hatred against foreigners, Jews and refugees. Already for this reason I have the desire to do my best to leave this neighbourhood and to find accommodation somewhere else- but- still I could not find anything'.*

The problem dragged on until July, with Wilfrid facing an angry neighbour and a tenant who was struggling to find accommodation for boys badly hurt by their experience of Nazi Germany. Some weeks later Dr Marks finally moved the hostel elsewhere.

'The letting has not been altogether a success', commented Wilfrid. It may not have been popular with one neighbour, but it may have

been very successful for the boys in need of help. Some months later, Dr Marks and his daughter left Britain for America.

Business & Austerity

Austerity continued for the rest of the decade, and well into the 1950s. Church's China was selling goods of low value, but great bulk. Wilfrid wrote of receiving a container from one small supplier, T.G. Green of Derbyshire, weighing two and a half tonnes.

Wilfrid might not have been selling what he wanted to sell, but business was still good. *'Money is still plentiful'* he wrote in October 1946 *'and it seems that customers are more apt to complain of the low prices of articles than grumble at goods being expensive'*. He told the Chronicle and Echo *'Such articles as pudding basins and tea plates are in greatest demand, and large numbers of people asking for articles in short supply have to be turned away. Some of the stuff is terrible. People would do better to hold off buying it than to have the stuff on their hands'*.

Post war taxation was high; in December Wilfrid wrote a cheque for £4,105 'excess profits' tax. *'The biggest cheque I have ever written'* he commented. Far from improving with the end of the war, supplies became even more scarce. All decorated china was produced exclusively for export, while the potteries were affected by the shortage of coal to fire the kilns. The business was forced to diversify and in July 1946 a large consignment of pyrex glass attracted customers.

In 1947 Wilfrid dismissed 'sensationalist' stories 'that crockery stocks will only last a few weeks'. *'Stocks are certainly low, and the supplement of stocks by manufacturers may soon be rather slower, but this does not mean that they will only last a few weeks'*, he told a Chronicle and Echo reporter. He pointed out that the pottery industry was a large contributor to the export drive. *'A percentage, very inadequate no doubt is being distributed to the home trade under the depressing category 'utility'…. Harassed retailers do what they can to distribute their small allocations fairly, generally giving first priority to their regular customers....* He ended on an optimistic note: *'Factories are being re-conditioned and manufacturing methods better organised; this should bring a steady improvement and healthy hope for the future.'*

In October 1946 the 'Pottery Gazette and Glass Trade Review' carried an article celebrating Wilfrid's 50 years in business. In that article Wilfrid admitted that he could not put any precise dates on the foundation of the business or its move to Northampton. So, in 1950 the business celebrated its centenary seven years too early. 'The Chronicle and Echo wrote *'When Britain was holding its Great Trades Exhibition at Crystal Palace in 1851; when crinolined women were decking out their Victorian cabinets... Mr. Thomas Church, an experienced local connoisseur of pottery and glass, decided to open a business on the Parade Northampton'*. It was actually Mr Chapman who celebrated the Great Exhibition with an award-winning Minton dinner service. It would be another twenty-one years before Thomas Church moved to Northampton.

The Chronicle and Echo continued: *'Even to walk through the showrooms at Church's... is a thrilling experience for lovers of beauty, colour and design and although one may join with Mr. Church in deploring the temporary sacrifice to export of so much of Britain's best in modern pottery and glass there still remains enough to delight the eye, particularly among the export rejects. It is these items, all of them aesthetic delights, that afford the hope of things to come when present austerity is eased and those beautiful British products once more flow back to the home market.'*

By 1948 it wasn't clear if Church's China would remain in the family. Vivian was expected to pursue a career in agriculture. Wilfrid, as he grew older, mulled over the options in his diary.

'It has been in my mind to make some drastic plan about my future position. As the twenty-one year agreement on the lease has now been fixed I am considering whether it would be advisable to dispose of the business, to have someone to manage it, to employ further qualified assistants and remain in it with less work or what to do.'

An advertisement in 1950.

The question was resolved, at least for the time being, with the arrival of Peter Andrews. Peter was the son of the family living next door, he had been the best man at Phil's wedding. In September 1949 he started work for 10s a week, spending the rest of his working life as an invaluable manager of the shop.

From 1945 to 1951 the annual turnover rose steadily from £15,583 to £20,947. In 1950, Wilfrid ceased to run the business as a self-employed sole trader. Church's China became a Limited Company, with the full title of Church's Glass and China Stores (Northampton) Ltd, to distinguish it from the continuing business in Devon. Wilfrid and Naomi were the only shareholders.

Improvements in trading conditions were slow to come. In 1952, on one of his regular trips to the Potteries, Wilfrid found that things were changing. China manufacturers were 'placing themselves in the position' to take orders from the home trade while the earthenware suppliers *'gave us to understand that with certain patterns, the choice was ours to give whatever quantities we desired.'*

In 1953 Wilfrid was still complaining of the difficulty in getting the stock he required, particularly from the *'traditional and reputable suppliers such as Wedgwood, Doulton and Copeland'* due to the export drive and the shortage of labour.

In 1945, against Wilfrid's advice, Miss Slade entered into a partnership to run Church's China Paignton with Mr Coates, a representative for Stoke on Trent manufacturers in the South West. With the business still trading under the name of Church's China, Wilfrid continued to take an interest. The partnership didn't work out; by 1956, Miss Slade had lost interest and she retired to live with her sister in Bradford-on-Avon.

The business continued under the ownership of Mr Coates until 1960 and carried on trading until 1991. Today It is still fondly remembered by the people of Torbay.

Prosperity

Despite the austerity of the 40s and early 50s, Wilfrid's personal finances prospered. He spent little on luxuries for himself and Naomi. Abstention from alcohol and tobacco helped them save, but they didn't live an extravagant lifestyle by middle class standards. In addition to the business, Wilfrid received income from his properties and investments.

He did indulge in a couple of luxuries. In 1949 he bought a Jowett Javelin car, itemising the costs in his diary: -

Car £750
Purchase Tax £209 1s. 8d
Delivery charge from Bradford £4 10s
Number plates £2
Road licence £8 15s
Total £974 6s 8d

'This is a huge figure and represents quite a luxury car, am rather surprised at my rashness in purchasing this especially as petrol is so difficult to obtain.'

A few weeks later he noted that this plus an income tax demand *'have both caused a considerable overdraft at the bank'.*

The second luxury was a television. On December 1st, 1949 the TV aerial was installed, but it was another two weeks before the broadcasting station at Sutton Coldfield was functioning. On Christmas Eve he watched a nativity play from Coventry, but at the same time Naomi was listening to the festival of nine lessons and carols on the radio. *'We have many luxuries now that we are likely to be confused in our interests'* he wrote.

These luxuries were little compared with the amount Wilfrid spent on supporting his three children and their partners. Joy and Leslie's business struggled to support the costs of a large house in Tunbridge Wells, and Wilfrid helped out with the move to a new property. Irene gave birth to a second child, Jonathan, in 1949. Her husband Henry set up a chemical business in Manchester. Wilfrid helped with that too, but the marriage was not successful. When they separated, Irene moved to live next door to her sister in Tunbridge Wells, her father once more on hand to help with the costs. One of his biggest outlays in support of his family though was to buy a farm in mid Wales to help Viv in his ambition to be a farmer.

Vivian Church

With the war over, Viv's training in South Africa as an RAF navigator was never put to the test in active service. Post war training in driving tractors and heavy vehicles may have had some use for his agricultural ambitions, but apart from that, he was keen to end his military service and begin a career in agriculture. His father appealed to the newly elected MP for Northampton, Reginald Paget and the director of Seal Hayne College. Between them, they lobbied the authorities to seek Viv's demobilisation so he could return to his interrupted course in agriculture. Finally, in August 1946, just before his 23rd birthday, he came home with his civvy suit to a celebratory meal with his parents.

The following year, he passed his exam in agriculture, and started two years teaching at Langley, a boys' boarding school in Norfolk. In 1949 he started a course at Emmanuel College, Cambridge with a view to working in agriculture overseas. While on a walking holiday in the Alps he met Valerie Bryant, and in June 1950 they were married, with the expectation that they would soon be stationed in Africa, probably Kenya, where he would be employed on major agricultural projects.

The wedding of Vivian Church and Valerie Bryant June 1950.

In August 1950, Wilfrid and Naomi set off on one of their regular holidays to Wales. They stayed at Bryn Tanat, a vegetarian guesthouse in Montgomeryshire. Picking up the local paper they saw a 115 acre farm for sale. The agent, a brother of the local MP Clement Davies, gave them the directions to the remote farm a few miles from Lake Vyrnwy called The Rhos, Dolanog. Wilfrid said it was Naomi's idea, *'really I cannot imagine Viv and Val settling down in such an out of the way district as this'*, he commented. So began the Church family's association with the community of Dolanog in the heart of mid Wales that continues to this day.

Colonial office uncertainty led to Vivian and Valerie re-thinking their plans, and the offer of support in buying a farm was attractive. On the 18th September Wilfrid, Vivian and Valerie attended the auction in the Royal Oak Hotel in Welshpool and found themselves the owners of a 115-acre farm bought for £5,000.

The farming community of Dolanog was predominantly Welsh speaking. Families had lived on the land for generations, never moving far from their home. It wasn't an easy life. Mains electricity and telephones had yet to arrive. Tractors were only just replacing horses, and upland farming was a hard, manual job. The nearest town was 15 miles away, and the young couple knew nobody. They were welcomed into a local community that taught them the practical aspects of running a farm that years at an agricultural college could never teach. Viv and Valerie's first two children, Katie and Philip were born on the farm in 1951 and 1953.

In October 1953, the farm had, according to Wilfrid, '400 sheep, 52 cattle, about a dozen pigs, poultry such as hens, cocks, ducks, drakes, geese, ganders, turkeys not to mention cats and a dog.' The work was hard, and the income was small. Wilfrid was getting older, with no-one in the family apart from Viv who could take over the business. John Roberts, who had been the farm help, was employed as a farm manager and in 1954 Viv and Valerie returned to Northampton with their two small children.

Wilfrid and Naomi refurbished the upstairs flat at No 20 Abington Park Crescent for the young family, and in March 1954 Viv started work at Church's China. The fourth generation had joined the business.

Two more children were born, Stephen in 1955 and Richard in 1958. In 1960 the family moved into a house of their own, just three doors further down the road at 22a Abington Park Crescent. Wilfrid and Naomi, now approaching their eightieth birthdays, looked for a smaller house. They moved to the flat at Number 20, with its spacious rooms overlooking Abington Park, while Number 18, their home for the last 37 years, was sold.

Keeping up the causes

Age did not dim Wilfrid's commitment to the causes that he, his father and brother, had championed for their whole lives. Causes such as vegetarianism, healthy eating, abstinence from alcohol and anti-vivisection seemed unfashionable as post war austerity gave way to a consumer boom.

Wilfrid had inherited his father's shareholding in Northampton Temperance Hall, sited on the corner of Princes St. and Newland, where the Grosvenor Centre now stands. In 1946 he became a director, as his father had been fifty years previously. The hall had been built in 1888 to promote total abstinence from alcohol, providing meeting rooms and social facilities where alcohol was expressly forbidden.

During the first world war the Temperance Hall became one of Northampton's early cinemas. An advertisement in 1915 boasted that it was home to 'The Picture Pioneers of Northampton' calling itself an electric theatre. Cinema became the main purpose of the building, and its intention to fight the scourge of alcohol became secondary. Wilfrid attended regular directors meetings, usually with little business to discuss, and came away with a small director's fee.

'This is an investment which brings in quite a good return' he wrote *'but not on account of its temperance work but because a poor type of film, appreciated by youngsters, gives thrilling and impossible accounts of cowboys, crime etc. Youth can take a great dose of this horror production without any lasting harm, that is how it seems to me.'*

By the 1960s, with the rise of television, cinema was on the decline. The Temperance Hall directors struggled to find other profitable uses for the building, it was put up for sale in 1963. Wilfrid and Vivian attended the auction with a view to putting in a bid if the reserve of £10,000 was not met, but it was sold for £15,000. Wilfrid attended the last shareholders meeting, noting in his diary the original purpose of the Temperance Hall Company *'...but now such work seems to have sunk away and the alcoholic drink is becoming more and more prevalent.'* Wilfrid received £992 from the winding up of the company. He was determined that the original purpose of his family's investment should not be forgotten and donated it to temperance causes. The building became a bingo club before it was demolished in 1973 to make way for the Grosvenor Centre.

Rationing had forced people to reduce their consumption of meat. The vegetarian movement claimed an upsurge of interest after the war. An article in the Northampton Independent on December 21st, 1951 headed 'Meatless Christmas for them', featured Wilfrid, his photographer friend Henry Cooper and Leslie Wiggins, who had been a conscientious objector with William Church in the First World War. The article reported that there were 438 registered vegetarians in Northamptonshire who were entitled to a ration of an extra 12 ounces of cheese and four ounces of margarine instead of meat.

Wilfrid chaired some well attended meetings of a group called the Health Freedom Society, which, as well as diet, covered issues relating to exercise and prevention and cures for various illnesses. One meeting, with 120 people attending at the Carnegie Hall (upstairs in Northampton library), was addressed by his son in law, Leslie Korth, on the subject of 'what it means to grow up'.

The Northampton anti-vivisection society had faded away, but Wilfrid continued to write occasional letters. In October 1947 he wrote a very short letter to the Empire Cancer Campaign '*The practice of vivisection has been so general in this research work and has reached such horrifying dimensions that I positively refuse to make any contribution.*' In 1954 he wrote to fundraisers for the Christian Medical College Hospital in Vellore, India, cancelling his regular contribution for the same reason.

The Rotary Club continued to play an important part in Wilfrid's life. He enjoyed the weekly lunch followed by a guest speaker and appreciated the rotary values of friendship and public service. He was president of the Northampton Rotary Club for the year 1948/49, requiring him to chair the weekly meeting and act as the club's spokesman. One of his tasks was to oversee the sorting and delivery of clothes sent by a club in Canada for needy Northampton residents. He was delighted when, on his return to Northampton, Viv joined Rotary. In 1972 Wilfrid proudly saw his son take office as President.

The arrival of television led to a new cause for letter writing. Very early on Wilfrid found that not all the BBC's output met his strict standards of taste and decency. His first letter of complaint in February 1950, addressed to Alexandra Palace, described the Saturday evening entertainer Vic Oliver as *'unfit for any decent audience.'* In another letter he complained about a children's programme: – *'It is not considered good manners for a speaker to retain a pipe between his teeth when speaking, or to use expressions such as 'great big'.*

In July 1954 he wrote to the popular entertainer Wilfrid Pickles objecting to the use of alcohol in a programme. There is no record of a reply. A letter to the BBC in 1966 complained *'Every programme has the raised glass, the tipped tankard, the bottle etc. ... The effects of such acting cannot but be harmful and give a decidedly bad interpretation of life. Less of the bar scenes, the cocktail party and alcoholic indulgences generally would give a more healthy view of life.'* The BBC replied that it would not be practicable to place a ban on all references to drink *'but a careful watch is kept on this matter to see that the bounds of reason are not overstepped.'*

Not surprisingly 'Till Death us do Part' did not meet his approval. He wrote to the BBC in January 1967 *'This production was one of the most unwholesome plays you have shown. It was dirty and obscene...'*

One belief handed down through the generations of the Church family did fade, and that was the strong Christian non-conformist tradition. Since long before the second world war, Wilfrid had not viewed himself as a member of any Church. Naomi, who like Wilfrid, came from a non-conformist family, regularly attended the Congregational Church in Abington Avenue, which later became the United Reformed Church. Wilfrid would sometimes attend with her, but more often he preferred to enjoy his Sunday mornings with a long walk.

'I never now feel encouraged or swept away by organised religion' he wrote in 1939. In 1942, feeling guilty about not accompanying Naomi to chapel he wrote *'Somehow I am not comfortable in the buildings that are called places of worship...'.* Another diary entry, in 1940, commented on a visit to Worcester: – *'The cathedral flourishes its architectural beauty but like those cities that possess such edifices*

they seem to have had their own pride and strength sapped in order to supply power to a religion.'

Later his diary entries on religion became more explicit. In 1954 he made the following entry.

> *'The Christian churches emphasise the divinity of Christ and to this belief I am not willing to agree although the life of Christ has a strong exampling power. I am sure there is a power around us all which can inspire us to good thoughts high ideals and what might be termed a Godliness.*
>
> *'But I cannot honestly accept a creed blindly and so it would seem that I must remain as one who thinks freely, who is willing to be open to conviction and who realised that there is progress even in thought although righteousness, human morality and the human being remain static and steadfast under many changing environments.'*

His loss of a conventional Christian faith took him very close to humanism. At a time when denying a religious faith was still quite an unusual position to take, and with Naomi's religious conviction remaining firm, he shared these thoughts only with his diary.

Retirement

Wilfrid occasionally talked of retirement. The arrival of Peter Andrews in the business, and later Vivian, meant he and Naomi could spend longer periods on holiday. In 1950 he went on another trip organised by Bassett-Lowke, this time to Switzerland, but from now on they spent more time at Wyndcroft in Devon. In 1960 he and Naomi enjoyed most of the summer there. The day to day management of the business was left to Viv and Peter Andrews. When in Northampton, Wilfrid continued to visit the shop most days for an hour or two, he would count the daily takings and prepare them for payment to the bank. He wrote: *'To be cut off entirely* [from the business] *would*

Wyndcroft. The holiday home in Devon

be a grievous break and to be able to enter and depart from the shop according to my inclinations is much to my liking.'

Time was taken up with other leisure pursuits. Wilfrid became a member of Northampton Bowls Club, and as he grew older, he began to write and reminisce more about his family and his youth. He started to research his family's ancestry. In 1959 he visited East Ilsley in Berkshire, where his father was born and, in search of more information, exchanged letters with the local vicar. He found the basic facts about his father and grandfather, but without the resources we have today, he was never able to find the details of his family's history which are now readily available from online historical sources.

During the 1960s Wilfrid read and transcribed his brother William's diaries (sadly disposing of all but the part relating to the first world war). He wrote a short booklet about the history of the business, which was given to family and friends, but was not available for sale. It provided material for several articles in the local newspapers and the pottery trade press and was an invaluable source for the early chapters of this book.

As Wilfrid and Naomi grew older, their circle of friends declined. Bassett-Lowke died in 1953 and his vegetarian friend, the photographer

Henry Cooper was gone too. With more time on his hands, the diary entries became longer, with the content focussed primarily on his three children and nine grandchildren. Vivian and Valerie were living three doors away, so he and Naomi saw their four children regularly. The grandchildren took it turns to be spoilt by Granny and Grandpa for Sunday lunch and Joy and Irene also visited regularly with their children. Joy's daughter Christine and Irene's daughter Phyllida both worked at Church's China for a short time.

Wilfrid and Naomi's diamond wedding September 1971
with their three surviving children Joy (left) Vivian and Irene.

Expanding the business

Church's China, unlike other successful independent China and Glass businesses, never owned the premises they traded from. The future beyond the expiry of the current lease was always uncertain. In 1960, Wilfrid and Vivian were conscious that their lease had only another ten years to run when they learned that the Emporium Arcade was to be sold by auction.

Wilfrid calculated that if he could buy the arcade for £50,000, with an interest rate of 6%, the investment might be worthwhile. He sought advice and learned there were concerns about the physical state of the arcade. There might need to be a large outlay in the future, so the idea was dropped, and the building was bought by a London property company for £55,750.

No 11 The Parade had suited Church's China well for fifty years. Its prominent position overlooking the Market Square could not be missed, but space on the ground floor was very restricted, with customers needing to be taken two floors up in the lift or down steep stairs into the labyrinthine basements. Turnover during the 1950s had doubled from £21,000 to £44,000, but by 1965, there had been little further growth. Physical space was needed for further expansion.

The opposite side of the arcade entrance was occupied by the London Liverpool and Globe Insurance Company. In 1962, they moved, opening up the possibility of expansion. Initial enquiries were rebuffed, but Vivian persevered. One problem was that the lease only had seven years to run, making a large investment on refurbishment a risk, so the idea was put on hold. There were other options. The former Admiral Rodney Pub premises on the west side of the Market Square extended right through to the Drapery. For 3,500 a year rent this seemed a good proposition, but the plans came to nothing when the building was let to a bank. It also seemed that the option of No.10 The Parade was closed off when, despite Viv's objection, an appeal was won to turn it into a betting shop, but that was only a temporary setback.

In July 1965 occupation of No. 10, The Parade was at last secured, together with a new lease for No. 11 giving the business some security for the future. Wilfrid thought that £5,000 would have to be spent on alterations. While number 11 had the use of the whole of the second floor of the Arcade frontage, No. 10 had the first floor with wide stairs leading up from the back of the ground floor shop. The two could be connected by the old lift, now stopping at the first floor which it used to pass.

The new shop was opened by Sir John Wedgwood on 29th November 1965. '*Speaking personally, I was very impressed even to a deep feeling of sentimentality and had to hold myself in*' wrote Wilfrid. The expansion enabled the shop to give more space to modern china and glass, together with some diversification into stainless steel and cookware, while upstairs there was space to properly display the huge range of tableware on offer.

Wilfrid expected to see a 50% growth in turnover to justify the costs and the new overheads. That happened quickly, with turnover growing initially to £70,000 in 1966 and then, in the following years, to over £100,000 in 1970.

Emporium Arcade after the expansion of Church's China.

Expanding Northampton

In 1968, the town with a history stretching back over one thousand years officially became a New Town. Plans emerged for rapid expansion to accommodate the thousands of new residents and new businesses that were expected. It took much longer than was originally envisaged for the town to grow from 130,000 to over 200,000, but growth did come, and with it, new demands on the town centre.

A Development Corporation was established to oversee the growth, with a specific remit to support the growing population by providing infrastructure and housing on the edge of town. Northampton Town Centre, with a road pattern that reflected its medieval history, was left for the Borough Council to redesign.

The Emporium Arcade stood on the edge of Newland, one of the most densely populated parts of the town centre. Its narrow streets of small Victorian terraced houses were interspersed with shoe factories. If Northampton was to have the modern shopping facilities required for a town of a quarter of a million people, then this would inevitably be the place to provide it.

In October 1968 the Emporium Arcade was for sale once more, and this time the Borough Council bought it. The Chronicle and Echo reported that the area, described as 'Action Area One' was destined for the development of a new covered market linked to a bus station and shopping street. The report suggested that the existing fish and meat market would be relocated, just as was proposed seventy years earlier, releasing the covered market on the corner of Sheep St for office development. It continued: –

'It is understood that the Corporation may start negotiating to buy the lease of Church's China Stores. Most of the other leases are due to expire shortly. Mr Vivian Church of Church's China Stores said today "We have had no official notification from the landlords, and we have had no approach from the Corporation regarding our lease. As far as we are concerned, we are here for

*another 42 years which is the extent of our lease. We have been
on this site for 130 years and we are most anxious to remain
here."*

Including a gap of 10 years, the business had actually been on the site
for only 95 years. Once again, the vague knowledge of the business's
history led to an exaggerated claim for its age.

Formal notice to quit the Emporium Arcade was received in
December. Church's China Stores needed to be out by the end of
December 1971; the 45 year-long lease, agreed when the business
expanded to both sides of the arcade entrance, would be terminated.
Other than for Church's China Stores, the Arcade had never worked
well commercially. It was on a slope, with small shops and studios.
Further space on the first-floor balconies was little used. It finished in
a dead end, so apart from an arm that led into Newland it provided
no connecting pedestrian route. However, it did provide affordable
space for small shops in the heart of the town. During the 1960s the
low rents and short leases had attracted several small arts, fashion and
music shops. These traders, working together with those interested
in the heritage of the town, formed a popular coalition against the
demolition plans.

Mr Harrison, who ran a music shop in the arcade told the Mercury
and Herald *'Local people just won't be able to run shops any longer. The
whole of the town centre will become multiple shops and the money will
be taken out of Northampton.'* That view was repeated by other arcade
traders.

In 1969 Vivian wrote an article in the journal of Northampton
Chamber of Trade in a similar vein.

*'Careless planning involving the wholesale and uncontrolled
disposal of valuable town centre sites to large development
companies, can lead to the virtual exclusion of local retailers
from the premier shopping areas of a new town. Thus, we may be
left with the ghastly prospect of a town centre- similar to many*

to be seen throughout the country- comprising multiple stores, supermarkets, chain shops, interspersed with innumerable banks and building societies. A gruesome picture of dull uniformity.' Whatever happened, Vivian's biggest fear was indecision and delay. *'We retailers and our customers need and deserve to know what we can expect in the future. Prolongation of the agony by the granting of short leases on existing premises is no good – at least five years is needed so that we may refurbish and improve our shops. With this in mind the planners should meet us individually to discuss our hopes and fears.*

'My most sanguine thoughts are of a fine new Northampton retaining its ancient individuality and at the same time incorporating a vigorous new shopping centre unlike, and much better, than any other in the country.'

With just that objective in mind, campaigners drew up alternative plans that incorporated the Emporium Arcade into the new Grosvenor Centre and bus station development, making the connections that the arcade had never made before.

The Borough Council was determined to press ahead with its plans. Over the next three years, Grosvenor Estates acquired the entire area between Lady's Lane, the Market Square, Abington St and Wood Hill. Their plan was to build a new covered shopping centre to meet the demands of national retailers.

Vivian, with his father's support, started the search for new premises. Finding somewhere with a prime town centre position together with enough storage space for the huge range of tableware stocked would be difficult. One property in Abington St seemed suitable, but eventually it fell through.

The media interest in the Market Square developments meant that the reminiscences of an old man who was born there and worked there all his life were invaluable. Wilfrid was the Chronicle & Echo's 'go to' man for nostalgia. One story he gave them was about the pair of handcuffs used to arrest the notorious criminal Captain Slash, handed down from his great grandfather John Spencer. It was great copy for the Chronicle and Echo and appears in Chapter Two of this book.

Memories didn't make Wilfrid sentimental about buildings that had been familiar to him for all his life. On October 22nd, 1970 the Chronicle and Echo published a letter from him reminiscing about his time working in Welsh House in the 1890's.

'There was nothing there that I understood as being of architectural or intellectual attraction. Really, I am indifferent as to what the planners decide to do with the old building.

As to the Market Square I am certain this should be conserved as far as possible in its present unique setting- a four cornered space, in the midst of modern new erections of steel and concrete.'

Campaigners wanted none of this steel and concrete. In May 1971 an action group was formed to save the arcade, and a petition was launched, rapidly collecting over 10,000 signatures. Vivian gave more positive support to the campaign, making clear that Church's China would prefer to stay put.

The campaign won national attention. In September the renowned architect and broadcaster Ian Nairn came to Northampton to make a film for TV about the threatened demolition that can still be watched online. He commented on how the frontage complemented many of the older buildings of the square. He walked along the arcade's deserted balconies, pointing out what could be done, challenging the claim that the building was of little architectural merit.

In October, hecklers were ordered out of a council meeting while Ron Dilleigh, leader of Labour opposition on the council was speaking in support of the demolition of the arcade. Labour and Conservative councillors united to support demolition, with just one councillor, Alderman John Poole speaking in support of a proposal to keep the frontage and demolish the rest. Alderman J.T. Lewis, Chairman of the Town Expansion Committee replied that the arcade *'was not in any stretch of the imagination a building of architectural merit.'* The Leader of the Council Alderman Corrin added *'I hope and believe myself that what is intended to be put there will be a vast improvement on what is there at the present time.'* Complaints that there would be no space for small independent shopkeepers were addressed with a promise of provision for about 25 small shopkeepers in the new Grosvenor Centre. This came to be known as 'The Friary', it was not a success and after a few years it was absorbed into Beatties Department Store.

The tenants were given another three months to quit; they were to vacate by the end of March 1972. Vivian's search for a single large property with showroom and storage space had come to nothing. A property was available on the Drapery, it wasn't big enough for the whole shop, but it was in a good position, so he took it. It was open for Christmas trading in December 1971, and was used for more modern tableware, kitchenware and gifts.

Finally, with little time to spare, a rather unlikely property became available in Sheep Street. It was a former garage, single storey, and with a large floorspace. It wasn't in an ideal position but would only be temporary. With little expense to convert it, Vivian took it and with days to spare the remainder of the business moved.

The north side of the Market Square with Welsh House, before restoration, on the right.

Just a few yards from the Emporium Arcade stood Welsh House. The building where Wilfrid Church had worked as an apprentice chemist over seventy years previously had lost its gabled roof with Collyweston slates. The mellow Northamptonshire sandstone walls were hidden by pebbledash and flaking paint. The ground floor was shared by a taxi business with a garage door front and Ruth Tuckey's sweet shop. It was to be swept away for a Market Square entrance for the Grosvenor Centre. If there was a campaign to save it, it was barely noticed alongside that for the Emporium Arcade.

The final hope of the Action Group was that the Emporium Arcade would be saved by a government inspector. Despite all the campaigning, this was not to be, the arcade was to be demolished and the date was set for work to start on April 4th, 1972.

There was one surprise though. The Inspector ordered that the façade of Welsh House must be restored. However, it turned out that little of the original could be saved and what stands there today is a reconstruction of Welsh House as it appeared over 100 years earlier.

Some parts of the Emporium Arcade were saved. Maybe more of it survives than the original Welsh House. The Chronicle and Echo reported on 26th April 1972 that '*Northampton Salvage Corps have arranged for the main entrance archway and possibly the balcony over it to be dismantled for re-building elsewhere, although no new home has been found for it yet.*' The report continued '*The sections will be numbered and will be transported free of charge by Wrefords the haulage firm. The services of Towcester Road Boys club have been volunteered to unload the lorry and stack the sections for storage*'. Where it is now is a mystery, both the lift and the cast iron range in the basement were transported to Abington Park Museum and could be seen there for many years.

The Northampton born journalist Matthew Engel, then a junior reporter for the Chronicle and Echo, wrote in his book 'Engel's England',

'*Despite a 10,000-signature petition, the logicians won. Down it came: Nat Bloom the Tailor, Harrison's records, Roy Douglas stamps and all. And the café where the reporters from the evening paper, the Chronicle and Echo- which had the building next door – would go for the mid-morning moan before the lunchtime moan in Shipman's. ...*

'*For the sentimentalists were not just right, but spectacularly right. Given a rear entrance and a refurb, the Emporium Arcade would have been Northampton's central attraction: a place of boutiques and galleries and vibrant enterprise.*'

CHAPTER EIGHT

THE TIDE FLOWS ON

'AND SO, THE TIDE FLOWS ON' WAS THE FINAL SENTENCE IN MY grandfather Wilfrid's diary. It was written on September 26th, 1973. A few days earlier he had been told by the doctor that little could be done to help him. Maybe it was deliberately written as his final words. He lived for another month, dying at home on 27th October aged 91.

In the last year of his life, he was proud to see Viv elected President of Northampton Rotary Club. He saw that the old Welsh House had been demolished, and Viv showed him plans being drawn up for Church's China to move into the new building.

Naomi continued to live at No 20a Abington Park Crescent, living alone for several more years until she needed regular personal care. She continued to love the theatre, often attending alone, and kept herself healthy with a daily walk in Abington Park. On one occasion, explaining a visit to St. Christopher's Old People's Home, she said she wanted to 'see what it was like to be old'. She died in February 1987; a few weeks short of her 104th birthday.

To everybody's surprise, the two temporary shops in the Drapery and Sheep Street were remarkably successful. They worked together well, the smaller Drapery shop, in a prime position, being used to

Naomi Church aged over 100 with one of her great grandchildren.

direct customers to the larger Sheep St shop. Very soon the problem of selling expensive goods from a single storey former garage with skylights became apparent. Within a few weeks of opening, thieves entered through the roof and stole £4,000 worth of goods, requiring the installation of a troublesome new burglar alarm that triggered on the slightest movement inside the building. Turnover grew from £145,000 in the last year of the Emporium Arcade to £207,000 in 1974.

In 1975, the new Welsh House was completed. The new sandstone façade hides a concrete interior that is structurally part of the new Grosvenor Centre. The only distinctive interior item required by the planners was the oak staircase with turned

Church's China in Welsh House.

balustrades; a replica of a staircase that had been there before, but wider to accommodate the free flow of customers. The top floor housed the kitchenware department linked to a contemporary china and glass department, which, in turn, led customers out into the first floor of the Grosvenor Centre.

Welsh House commemorates Northampton's historic association with Wales. Before rail and modern roads, welsh drovers transported livestock across the country by foot, in huge convoys along well-trodden routes. They arrived in Northampton's market to sell their stock, or to rest awhile on their way to London. Some settled here, and maybe that is the origin of the building's name. Above the bay window, the wall is decorated in white stucco plaster, carrying the date 1595 and inscribed with the Welsh Motto 'Heb Dyw, heb dim, Dyw a Digon' Without God, without anything, God is enough. Coats of arms represent old Welsh families, with the red dragon clearly visible.

Welsh House was one of the few buildings to survive the great fire of Northampton in 1675, its stone construction enabling people to escape from the Market Square. The frontage though is that of a domestic residence, not of a modern retailer. One difficulty was always to persuade people to climb two stone steps and enter through a narrow doorway. The premises also suffered from precious little window space, critical to a retailer.

Once inside, the open plan floorspace worked well. Vivian used what was then a very unusual idea in the trade, allowing customers to roam over the stockroom to look at over 150 patterns of tableware.

The 1970s and '80s were great years for the china and glass retailer. Far removed from the austerity of the 1950s, people could now buy fine, decorated china and crystal for their homes. A formal dinner set for the dining room could be combined with a casual pottery or stoneware set for the kitchen. Homes were decorated with figurines, not just ceramic, but increasingly made from hand-painted resin, with collections and limited editions adding interest. During the first five years in Welsh House turnover doubled to over half a million. It then doubled again to over a million by the middle of the 1980s.

Church's China was a founding member of a prestigious buying group of similar retailers, around twenty throughout the country. Known as the Guild of Specialist China and Glass Retailers, they worked closely with key suppliers in developing mutually advantageous trading relationships, including the commissioning of exclusive products.

For the time being, Church's was able to compete successfully with multiple retailers. Department Stores opened rooms in their stores, operated by major Stoke-on-Trent manufacturers. A process of mergers had led to the UK ceramics sector being dominated by two large Stoke based groups, Wedgwood and Royal Doulton. Together with Royal Worcester & Spode, and Stuart Crystal leading for the cut glass industry in Stourbridge, these companies opened rooms in Beatties (later House of Fraser) and Debenhams (formerly Adnitts) in Northampton. Seventy years earlier Church's China survived alongside competition from up to five local china shops. Now, the main competitors were Church's own suppliers.

In the late 1970s the fifth generation arrived in the business. Philip Church opened what was initially an independent business in Banbury, operated in close collaboration with the Northampton store. In 1982 Stephen and I joined the Northampton business. All three of us had followed other paths before joining, but the lure of selling pottery is strong when growing up with it, working holidays and Christmas and talking shop at home.

In the 1980s, the future seemed very secure. Surely, people would always want to dine with good quality china and glass, and to decorate their homes with high quality ornaments. People would, it was thought, always want to see and touch what they are buying in a shop. Mail order was in its infancy, and only worked for a narrow range of goods.

With a strong brand name in Northamptonshire and beyond it was time for further expansion. Branches were opened in Rugby, Kettering and Peterborough with all three, plus Banbury, taking advantage of the Northampton store's depth of stock to offer a rapid service for the smaller towns. Turnover doubled again, reaching two million in 1991.

With three sons in his business, Vivian was able to spend more time on his greatest passion, recognised by his father since he was a little boy, fishing. Newly built reservoirs such as Grafham and Rutland water became the summer evening destination of choice. Gradually, my mother and father spent more time in their cottage in Wales, just half a mile

Vivian Church

from the farm they had lived in as a newly married couple.

This period was the heyday of retail. The value of prime retail properties rocketed, and landlords could expect ever rising rents. As the campaigners to save the Emporium Arcade feared, small independent retailers were mostly driven out of town centres simply because of property values. Leases themselves became assets, to be bought and sold because of the value of a retail location, but security was only as long as the length of the lease.

The 21-year lease on Welsh House expired in 1996. It was apparent that rents for such prime locations were unaffordable for businesses like Church's China. A shop with a strong local reputation could do well in what was viewed as a 'secondary' location. St Giles Street was chosen, and a lease was agreed with Northampton Borough Council for a building which had contained two small shops and a printing business. Space was cramped compared to Welsh House, but the overheads were massively reduced. After a few years the shop expanded into the premises next door to give more space to the cookshop with a tableware showroom upstairs.

Business was changing fast. A business that once depended on cups and saucers, plates and bowls for its trade now thrived on small collectable gifts. Tableware, which used to be the bread-and-butter of the business, began a slow decline.

The 1990s saw the arrival of the internet. Quick communications meant an opportunity for more business overseas. There was a large

Church's China in St. Giles St.

discrepancy in prices between Britain and USA. Americans loved traditional English china and glass, so this became an important source of new business. Throughout the 1990s, the Northampton shop and four branches continued to turn over £2 million a year, peaking at over £2.8 million in the year 2000. The millennium combined with the Queen Mother's 100th birthday made it a great year for collectors. The Queen's golden jubilee two years later crowned this commemorative time.

Within five years, changes which had been gradual for the last twenty years, suddenly became much faster. Modern lifestyles no longer had a place for traditional china and glass. The trend towards minimalism meant people were content to eat off plain white plates and clear crystal glasses. This, combined with modern production methods, meant that goods could be manufactured anywhere in the world, and the great manufacturers of Stoke on Trent were very quickly all but finished.

Retailers can diversify, and Church's did so with some success. One hundred years previously, W.T. Church had sold pudding basins and mixing bowls. Pottery and kitchenware had always been important to the business, that had expanded to saucepans, kitchen implements and all the elements of a modern cookshop. The giftware trade too become more diverse. Soft toys, jewellery, even chocolates were all tried with varying degrees of success.

Quite quickly, the trend in tableware happened in gifts too. People no longer wanted 'clutter'. Mantlepieces, even where they still existed, no longer carried dust-gathering ornaments. The power of great brand names no longer applied; simple, stylish goods could be manufactured far more cheaply abroad. Church's China adapted to this trend too, working with other retailers to source their own products in the Far East.

As the internet and mail order grew in importance, the physical shop ceased to be the only way to display goods. Church's successfully developed a website business that took a growing share of the turnover. Retail rents though continued to rise. The branches ceased to be profitable, and one by one they were all closed.

By 2005 it was clear that the business could no longer support three brothers. I left the business to concentrate on my work in local government, I had been Mayor of Northampton in 1997. Philip left a couple of years later.

During this time, Northampton town centre itself was struggling. People

Richard Church Mayor of Northampton 1997-8.

were willing to travel further to shop. The Grosvenor Centre met the demands of the 1970s and 80s but did not provide the large floor spaces with easy cheap parking that the multiple retailers and their customers were looking for. Key to updating Northampton's attempt to compete with Milton Keynes and out of town retailing was the need to redevelop and expand the Grosvenor Centre. That was effectively killed off both by the recession that began in 2008 and the further attraction of out of town shopping with the development of Rushden Lakes.

When the lease finished on the St. Giles St shop in 2011, Stephen had to downsize the business further, moving to a small shop in The Ridings Arcade. Web based business became increasingly important, but the damage caused to the business by the high overheads of previous years could not be undone, and the shop was closed in 2012. The internet side of the business was acquired by Peter Jones China of Yorkshire and lives on under the name of the UK Gift Company.

Church's China's final home, The Ridings Arcade.

The story of the end of Church's China is typical of many similar businesses. Almost all of the fellow members of the Guild of China and Glass Retailers have gone the same way. Most of the products that these specialist shops sold are now found only in antique shops and charity shops. They are just no longer made.

It is said that a family business usually lasts for just three generations. That Church's China lasted for five is in part a tribute to a family who have worked well together, never seeking to take more out of the business than it could afford and we have relied on excellent and loyal staff. However, nothing good lasts forever.

'The tide flows on' and fond memories are retained.

CHAPTER NINE

STORMS IN A TEACUP?

THERE'S NOTHING SPECIAL ABOUT THE CHURCH FAMILY.
Five generations of us have lived relatively comfortable and
unexceptional lives in a moderately large English Midlands town.

This book could have been called 'Where did it all go right', but
another Northampton man took that title for his book. Andrew Collins,
the writer and broadcaster, grew up in the 1970's, just a few hundred
yards from my family in Abington Park Crescent. He has written about
his fond memories of the town, and he shares with me, my siblings, my
parents and my grandparents an unexceptional childhood growing up
with loving parents in a safe and caring environment.

Two things about the Church family make the writing of this book
possible.

The first is that shopkeepers, particularly those that trade right
in the centre of a town, tend to be well known. What happens in and
around their business is likely to be noticed and reported in the local
press. That's been true for the Church family ever since they arrived
in the town in 1873 and stones were hurled through their windows
less than a year later. That happened because of where they lived, and
they lived where they did because of their trade. Such things happen
to shopkeepers and are remembered down the generations.

Amongst the most powerful memories of anyone's hometown are the long disappeared local shops. For thousands of people in Northampton their memories include Church's China. That is inevitable, and those collective memories are at the heart of any community. Unlike now, shops usually carried the family name of their owners, but what people remember is the name of the shop, not the people behind it.

The second, and bigger reason why this book is possible is that two members of my family wrote diaries. Everything from the most tragic to the most mundane is written down. Sometimes, when the great events of history are unfolding, I just wish they had written more. Most of the time, I wish they had written less. The precise details, to the minute, of great uncle William's long walks or my grandfather's daily report on his bees are of little interest to anyone but them. But they were personal diaries and they weren't written just for our benefit.

Two events which take a large part of this book clearly were not storms in a teacup for any family.

William's arrest for his refusal to fight in the First World War was exceptional, and the result of principles that set the family apart from others. Pacifism, vegetarianism and abstinence from alcohol were all part of a firm adherence to a linked set of values, elements of which are growing in importance today. Together with Liberal and Socialist politics my family were, and to a degree still are, a bit outside of the mainstream of middle-class urban life. They did not, with my wayward exception, seek to be politicians and they didn't seek fame or attention for how they lived and what they believed. My ancestors lived out their lives by the principles they thought were right, and they never sought attention or admiration for what they did.

The tragedy inflicted on my family by my uncle Philip's death in the second world war was also, sadly, unexceptional. The pain at the loss of a newly married son was shared by thousands, and his father's moving account of it speaks for many others. That it should happen to a pacifist father makes it particularly poignant, but no greater a loss than any son's death in war.

For the wider community of Northampton my family's overall story really is a storm in a teacup. We created ripples that extend a short distance in time and space, no more. The diaries shed light on the times in which they were written. The social history of Northampton and the events that the town's people have lived through can be described through the lives of mine and many other families.

That is why my family story is worth telling.

Index

People with the surname Church are not included in the index. All family members named in the book appear in the family tree. Other very frequently repeated places are also not included, such as Market Square and Emporium Arcade.